MATTHEW MEAD'S MONSTER BOOK OF
HALL WEEN

MATTHEW MEAD'S
MONSTER BOOK OF
HALL WEEN

TABLE   OF

contents

Time Inc. Home Entertainment
Publisher Richard Fraiman
General Manager Steven Sandonato
Executive Director, Marketing Services Carol Pittard
Director, Retail & Special Sales Tom Mifsud
Director, New Product Development Peter Harper
Assistant Director, Bookazine Marketing
Laura Adam
Assistant Publishing Director Joy Butts
Associate Counsel Helen Wan
Associate Manager, Product Marketing
Nina Fleishman
Design & Prepress Manager Anne-Michelle Gallero
Book Production Manager Susan Chodakiewicz
Special thanks Glenn Buonocore, Jim Childs,
Lauren Hall, Jennifer Jacobs, Suzanne Janso, Brynn
Joyce, Robert Marasco, Amy Migliaccio, Brooke Reger,
Ilene Schreider, Adriana Tierno, Alex Voznesenskiy,
Sydney Webber

Published by Time Inc. Home Entertainment

Time Inc.
1271 Avenue of the Americas
New York, New York 10020

ISBN 10: 1-60320-105-X
ISBN 13: 978-1-60320-105-6

Library of Congress Control Number: 2009928408

Time Inc. Home Entertainment is a trademark of
Time Inc.

Printed in the USA

We welcome your comments and suggestions.
Please write to us at:
Monster Book of Halloween
Attn: Book Editors
PO Box 11016
Des Moines, IA 50336-1016

If you would like to order any of our hardcover
Collector's Edition books, please call us at
1-800-327-6388 (Monday through Friday,
7:00 a.m.–8:00 p.m. or Saturday, 7:00 a.m.–
6:00 p.m. Central Time).

Downtown Bookworks Inc.
President Julie Merberg
Senior Vice President Pam Abrams
Design and Illustration Brian Michael Thomas
        OUR HERO PRODUCTIONS
Writers Sarah Egge, Carol Spier

Text and Design © 2009 Downtown Bookworks Inc.

Photography © 2009 Matthew Mead
Special thanks Sarah Parvis, Patty Brown,
LeeAnn Pemberton

AUTHOR'S ACKNOWLEDGEMENTS
I would like to thank everyone involved in creating
this monster Halloween edition, especially my wife
Jenny and my assistants Lisa Renauld and Lisa
Bisson. Sarah Egge provided amazing words and
hard work on this beautiful book. Sue Chandler and
her assistant Michelle lent their extraordinary baking
talents. Mary and Gordon Welch get special thanks
for all that they do for me. A big thanks go to our kid
cast: Jill Stoddard and her children Isabelle, Bret, and
Michael, as well as their cousin and kind neighbor.
Linda MacDonald, my favorite blogger from
restyledhome.blogspot.com continues her amazing
support for my brand. Thanks to everyone at
Downtown Bookworks and to our amazing designer
Brian Michael Thomas. And to all of my fans who
continue to inspire me with their fresh ideas and
thoughtful notes. Happiest of Halloweens!

Notice: This book is intended as an educational and
informational guide. With any craft project, check
product labels to make sure that the materials
you use are safe and nontoxic. "Nontoxic" is a
description given to any substance that does not
give off dangerous fumes or harmful ingredients
(such as chemicals or poisons) in amounts that
could endanger a person's health. The recipes and
instructions in this book are to be followed exactly
as written. No party involved in the production of
this book is responsible for your specific health or
allergy needs that may require medical supervision
or for any adverse reactions to the recipes contained
in this book. The recipes and instructions in this
book are intended to be performed with adult
supervision.

Time to Celebrate!

Every season that comes to my small New England town is a delight, but I have a special fondness for autumn. In this community, Halloween is celebrated nearly the same way it was when I was a boy. Children excitedly debate their costume options; parents plan fun parties; and neighbors wrap their porches with festive decorations.

In this book, I capture the traditions of Halloween—the pumpkins, ghosts, spiders, and spooks—that continue to entertain us all. But I've given those familiar ideas a fresh spin. My goal is always to inspire you to bring these recipes, crafts, decorations, and party ideas into your homes. And I know how important it is to make it all easy, inexpensive, and quick to accomplish.

I've designed these projects so that with one trip to the craft shop or grocery store you can get all the supplies you need to whip up a season's worth of fun. Even closer to home, a walk in the neighborhood will turn up the materials for many projects. And don't underestimate the inspiration you'll find in your own attic or at a neighbor's garage sale. I never do!

Happy Halloween!

Matthew

Fast Fun

Crafts, decorations, and snack ideas that are a cinch to whip together.

halloween easy treats

They're creepy and they're kooky and, even better, these ideas are downright simple. With a few spare minutes, you can convert ready-made foods into special snacks or give your rooms a festive holiday dress up.

STICK FIGURE

Bring this handy treat to life with a face fashioned from orange candies. Insert a chocolate-covered pretzel into the side of a store-bought cupcake, such as a Hostess® Ding Dong®. Stick on orange M&M's® Minis®, Tic Tacs®, or Reese's Pieces® with small dabs of chocolate frosting.

TOOTHSOME TIBIAS

Form sugar-cookie dough from the grocery store into bone-shape cookies by using a cookie cutter. Frost them with white Royal Icing (page 242). When dry, outline them with a food-safe black marker from the craft store.

For cookie cutters, visit chandlerscakeandcandy.com.

TREAT DISPLAY

Flip a cake stand over to create a simple new
serving piece. Use the underside of the top
for candies and cookies, and place a candle in
the center of the stand. Dots of ready-made
black frosting form ghost eyes.

PUMPKIN COOKIES

Turn Nilla® Wafers into little, adorable, edible jack-o'-lanterns. Tint
white cake frosting orange using food color, then warm it in the
microwave on 50 percent power for 1 minute to soften. Drizzle frosting
over the cookies to coat completely. When dry, draw faces using black
food-safe markers.

spider bite

Assemble several chocolate delights into one amazing arachnid. Start with a dark chocolate dessert cup for the body, and fill it with ready-made chocolate mousse, piped from a decorating bag fitted with a 1M tip. Break chocolate-covered pretzels into pieces to use as legs. Use a chocolate truffle as a head and attach small candy icing eyeballs with a smidge of melted chocolate. A line of orange candies tops it off. Turn the serving plate into a webbed nest by using a bamboo skewer to draw lines of raspberry and mango dessert sauces. If desired, surround the plate with store-bought chocolate cookies dipped in melted chocolate (see "How to Melt Chocolate," page 242) then in orange nonpareils.

ritzy snake

Stretch out a line of Ritz® crackers and use peanut butter to join them into a delicious reptile snack. Decorate the body with yellow M&M's® Minis®. Black ball nonpareils, used to decorate cookies, become eyeballs and nostrils when held in place with peanut butter. Laffy Taffy® makes the tongue.

choco-smiles

Cut out a toothy jack-o'-lantern face from black tape, such as plastic electrical tape or fabric duct tape. Attach it to a foil-wrapped chocolate orange from the grocery store. Roll up a stem out of additional tape, and adhere it to the top of the orange.

THE EVIL EYE

Turn snappy green apples sinister with the addition of gummy eyeballs. Start with room-temperature apples (cold ones will sweat and the decorations won't stick). Build eyeballs by starting with gummy fruit circles, then adding pupils and lash lines made from black ready-to-use fondant (a cake-decorating ingredient available at craft stores). Top them with a blob of white Royal Icing (page 242) and a dark-chocolate chip. Attach eyeballs to the apples using a dot of icing as glue.

SQUIRMY WORMS

To construct these yummy, nutty worms, cut a squiggle shape out of black card stock. Attach chocolate-covered almonds to the paper using melted chocolate (see "How to Melt Chocolate," page 242). Use piping gel to add candy icing eyes and red cookie-decorating dots.

brain freeze

Carve a daringly realistic brain out of a honeydew melon by using an X-Acto knife or paring knife to replicate channels in the rind. Then place it in a large mixing bowl. In a second bowl mix up four 3-ounce packets of strawberry-flavored gelatin according to package directions and pour over the melon until it is fully covered. Refrigerate overnight, then scoop out the melon with a large spoon or spatula. Scrape away some of the gelatin, as shown.

center stage

Build this tower of treats for the center of your buffet or dining table. Start with a cake stand embellished with silk leaves, acorns, and holiday candies. For the center pumpkin, cut off the stem and an inch of the top in a level line. Top the pumpkin with a dinner plate or platter weighed down with a smaller pumpkin and more treats.

GOT GHOSTS?

Decorate the side of drink glasses with black fabric tape or black electrical tape cutouts, then fill with milk.

say cheese!

Use mini-cupcakes as the staging ground for Halloween decorations. Adorn some with chocolate-covered peanuts in festive colors, and set a painted walnut jack-o'-lantern atop another. (See walnut instructions, page 102.)

trick-or-treat sticks

Go to matthewmeadstyle.com to download the wrapper pattern; print out as many as you will need. Remove the manufacturer's wrappers from candy sticks such as Sugar Daddy's®. Using a small pastry brush, paint the end of each candy stick with piping gel and sprinkle nonpareils over it (you'll find both at a cake-decorating store). Place a wrapper facedown on a work surface. Center a candy stick on the wrapper, fold the wrapper over the top, then fold in the sides. Secure with a little tape. Twist the wrapper bottom around the stick.

scary snack mix

The goblins will get you if you run out of this yummy party mix. Stir together 2 cups each caramel corn (store-bought or make your own from "Crunchy Caramel Corn" recipe on page 80), Reese's® Puffs cereal, waffle pretzels, peanut M&M's®, and mini Nutter Butter® cookies in a large bowl. You've now got 10 irresistible cups of snack mix. This mix is perfect for filling small treat bags, too.

spirit raisers

One look at these pumpkin-faced glasses and you'll feel silly.
One sip, you'll feel lightheaded.

For the decorated glasses, cut the jack-o'-lantern from black electrical tape. (Use the patterns on page 244 or create your own). Press the tape cutouts onto balloon-shape wineglasses or brandy snifters. For four 12-ounce cocktails, fill a pitcher with ice. Add ½ cup vodka, ½ cup orange liqueur (such as triple sec), 1 cup carrot juice, and 1 cup citrus energy drink (such as SoBe®). Stir to mix. Pour through a strainer into the decorated glasses. Garnish each with an orange slice if you like. For a kids' "cocktail," fill glasses with orange juice.

orange HOT CHOCOLATE

Get your cocoa into the spirit of the day by making it from white chocolate.

12 ounces premium white chocolate
8 cups milk
1 teaspoon vanilla extract
2 drops orange food color
Whipped cream and chocolate nonpareils, for garnish

1. Coarsely chop the white chocolate and transfer it to a medium-size heatproof bowl. Set aside.

2. Heat milk in a medium saucepan over medium heat until bubbles begin to form at edge of surface, about 4 minutes. Immediately pour milk over chocolate. Stir until chocolate is melted and mixture is smooth.

3. Whisk in vanilla and food color, then continue to whisk until a light foam forms on surface. Pour into ten mugs and garnish with whipped cream and chocolate nonpareils. Serve immediately.

Makes ten servings

DONUT HOLE KABOBS

Start with 20 donut holes and four 12-inch bamboo skewers. Melt ¼ cup of chocolate chips and place the melted chocolate in a plastic food storage bag. Snip a tiny piece from one corner of the bag and pipe droll faces onto four donut holes. Set aside on waxed paper.

Place ½ cup each of purple and orange candy sprinkles in separate dishes. With a small pastry brush, apply piping gel on the remaining donut holes, covering them entirely or in patterns as shown. Roll each donut hole in sprinkles. Set aside on waxed paper for 10 minutes.

Thread five donut holes, including one face, onto each skewer. If you wish, cut the sharp tip off each skewer with craft scissors before serving the kabobs.

FUNNY FACES

There's no carving required for these refreshing not-pumpkin heads, and they remain cute when you cut them up for serving. Just use a black food marker (found at a cake-decorating store) to draw whimsical or spooky faces on tangelos, oranges, or tangerines.

halloween QUICK TRICKS

Here are a handful of simple decorations to display year after year and others to set up and then pass out to friends and would-be tricksters. We supply the ideas and the graphics; you add candies, whimsy, and a dose of ghoulish imagination.

Give pantry goods a fun holiday makeover by taping on temporary paper labels. Make your own or download the ones pictured here from matthewmeadstyle.com. Out of the cupboard, they make eye-catching props for the kitchen counter.

57
KINDS OF BOB

CORN
OFF THE bOb

TINY TENDER KERNELS OF BOB

13 OUNCES

over 100 bat parts inside

BAT BITES

TINY PIECES OF MACERATED BAT

THE SAVORY TASTE
OF TRANSYLVANIA

aged 300 years

MONSTER MASH
that keep on tasting

MASHED BY THE FEET OF A
THOUSAND MONSTERS

stringed
fiends

magical chairs

Raid the linen closet for a white sheet to drape over an armchair. Cut ghost eyes from black construction paper and ahdere with double-stick tape.

WICKED POSY

Cast a spell over a single orange posy by cutting features out of black paper or electrical tape and tucking them into the center of the flower. Tie wire-edge ribbon to the stem.

THE FRIGHTFUL COUNTDOWN

Help children anticipate the holiday by counting down the 13 days before Halloween using this clever wall arrangement. Decorate treat bags from the craft store with numbers and sayings downloaded from matthewmeadstyle.com or those you create yourself. Affix the labels to the bags using double-stick tape. Trim the tops of the bags with scalloped scrapbooking scissors. Tuck in lightweight candy treats or toys to unwrap each day. And stick the bags on the wall with tape or Zots® clear adhesive dots, which are sold in the scrapbooking supply section of the craft store. (See the full arrangement on page 24.)

POST A COMMENT

Create a quick holiday decoration with Post-it® Super Sticky Notes in pumpkin colors. Use orange and green notes to form the gourd shape, then tape on black-construction-paper cutouts for the jack-o'-lantern face.

TAKE WING

Serve up a cup of hot cocoa in a mug decorated with a temporary bat motif. Cut the shape (you can use the pattern on page 244) out of black construction paper and attach it with double-stick tape.

trick-or-treat tower

A wire-basket tree makes a fun decorative accent that dispenses favors too. Fill small gift boxes with sweets or other treats; wrap them in black or orange paper, adding contrasting paper bands cut with scalloped-blade scissors. Tie each with rickrack, ribbon, or cord, adding a small trinket if you wish. Fill small crepe paper favor baskets with candies and hang them from the basket edges.

To order favor baskets, visit blumchen.com. For wire basket trees like this one, visit handcrafttexas.com (be sure to mention Matthew Mead's Monster Book of Halloween to avoid the normal $50 minimum purchase).

cast-a-spell mugs

Send a spooky message with mugs, glasses, or paper cups embellished with letters. Download the alphabet from matthewmeadstyle.com or create your own. Affix a single letter to each mug with double-stick tape or decoupage medium (such as Mod Podge®). Place a second letter on the opposite side of each mug to provide even more spelling options. Fill with candy and offer as party favors.

GIVEAWAY BOXES

These print-and-fold packages are as sweet as the candies or sentimental tokens inside. Download the patterns from matthewmeadstyle.com and print them onto medium-weight orange card stock. Following the guides, cut the patterns out. Fold each along the long lines; overlap the long side extensions and secure with double-stick tape or craft glue. Tuck in the flaps at one end, fill with tiny treats, and close the other end.

FRAMED MEMORIALS

Pay homage to the masters of creepiness with this eerie entryway decoration. Use ours as inspiration or choose your own Halloween-inspired words, numbers, or phrases. Write or print them on tea-colored paper, in an old-fashioned script or calligraphy font. Place in a purchased black collage frame (ours is from Target), or use in individual frames and hang them grouped together.

retro graphics wall ornaments

Trim a wire tree with small ornaments and trinkets from the holiday department at a craft store. You'll need beveled glass and scalloped-edge copper foil (from a stained-glass supply store), card stock, hot glue, and ribbon. Download the motifs here from matthewmeadstyle.com or choose your own, and print them out on card stock. For each ornament, cut out a motif to fit a glass piece. Cut a piece of copper foil ½ inch longer than the circumference of the glass. Place the glass on the cardstock and wrap the foil around the glass, tightly folding it over to hold the layers together. Use hot glue to attach a ribbon loop to the back of each ornament.

For a wire tree like this one, visit handcrafttexas.com (be sure to mention Matthew Mead's Monster Book of Halloween to avoid the normal $50 minimum purchase).

BLACKBIRD WREATH

Small beady-eyed blackbirds keep a woeful watch over this wreath. Begin with a 10-inch grapevine wreath; spray it with flat black paint. Arrange 7 faux blackbirds and 12 faux quail eggs on the wreath and affix with hot glue, tucking a few black marabou feathers under them as you do so. Add a few more feathers as you wish.

GLITTER JACK BASKETS
Whether you are collecting treats or passing them out,
a basket that sparkles with a ghoulish face is the ideal container.

Copy or scan and print the faces on page 245, then cut them out (medium-weight card stock works best). Spray a straw basket with flat black paint; let dry completely. Set the basket on its side. Attach the cutouts to the dry basket with quick-setting craft glue; let it dry completely. Spread decoupage medium (such as Mod Podge®) over one of the cutouts with a small paintbrush. Sprinkle with orange glitter (use a blend of oranges for a more fiery glow). Repeat for each remaining cutout. Let the cutouts dry completely before standing the basket upright. Gently remove any loose glitter with a clean paintbrush.

sweet treats

Recipes and embellishing ideas for delicious and creative goodies.

Haunted Cookie Houses

What do you get when you mix craft-store birdhouses with grocery-store cookies? A recipe for so-easy decorative houses! No need to build the structure—simply paint and embellish a wooden one to use as a base. Low-calorie snack packs provide the supplies for roofs, siding, and architectural details, and they allow for virtually guilt-free sampling along the way. But just like the witch's house in the story of Hansel and Gretel, these tempting structures are not for eating.

all a facade

Decorate a house-shaped wood cutout as a holiday door hanging. Paint the cutout with black acrylic paint and let dry. Use orange sanding sugar, affixed with brushed-on piping gel, to coat the house. Highlight the trim and windows using brown piping gel from wilton.com or a cake-decorating store, and add frosting or candy pumpkins. Hang the house from a ribbon tacked to its back with small nails.

Roof
Chips Ahoy!® Thin Crisps

Trim
Oreo® Fun Sticks

Roof peak
Golden Oreo® Mini Cakester

Planters
Oreo® Thin Crisps

ITTY-BITTY COTTAGE

Embellish a tiny house ornament in a jiff, using orange-tinted Royal Icing (page 242) to outline windows and doors and add a flower border. First, coat the craft-store house with black acrylic paint. To cut the cookies so they don't crumble, use a serrated knife.

Roof
HoneyMaid® Cinnamon Thin Crisps

Base
HoneyMaid® Cinnamon Roll Thin Crisps

TWO-STORY TOWER

Turn a birdhouse into a creepy nest for a large candy spider. To dress up an orange-painted house, use black-tinted Royal Icing (page 242) to pipe decorative patterns, borders, and stars. Adhere spider with a dab of icing.

Roof
Golden Oreo® Fun Stix

Base
Oreo® Thin Crisps, frosted and dipped in orange and black nonpareils

Windows
Nabisco® Classics Iced Lemon Shortbread

Spider
chandlerscakeandcandy.com

Bewitched Barn

With a large plywood barn as a base, you can set up a spooky farm scene. Paint the barn black, then decorate it with purple and white royal icing. Use Shredded Wheat® cereal as hay bales, sprinkle on black sanding sugar as dirt, and prop up sugar candies shaped like skeletons, jack-o'-lanterns, and black cats.

Roof
Nabisco® Classics Cocoa Creme Sandwich

Sugar Candies
chandlerscakeandcandy.com

HOUSE OF BRICKS

Add architectural charm to a tall, plain house by painting it black, then covering it with chocolate-cookie "bricks." Tucking in ghost and bat sugar candies, and piping on orange Royal Icing (page 242) provides Halloween novelty.

Roof
HoneyMaid® Cinnamon Thin Crisps

Bricks
New Morning® Mini Bites Chocolate
Graham Snacks (made by U.S. Mills)

Sugar Candies
chandlerscakeandcandy.com

crow's nest

An eerie wooden crow bobs above this black-painted house with a
sugar-candy witch at the doorstep. Coat the sides of the house with
black sanding sugar, affixed with brushed-on icing gel. Pipe on thick
orange icing gel to create dripping eaves. Black icing gel dots the
base and trims the roofline.

Roof
Planters® Peanut Butter
Cookie Crisps

Exterior
HoneyMaid® Cinnamon Roll
Thin Crisps

Base
Golden Oreo® Fun Sticks

sweet mutations

Starting with a favorite cookie from the grocery store, whip up some imaginative new holiday treats with these simple embellishment ideas. We used Pepperidge Farm® Soft Baked Snickerdoodles for the cookies pictured here, but you can select any soft-baked cookie that tickles your taste buds.

all-weather wicked

Using an umbrella-shaped cookie cutter—or wielding a paring knife with a steady hand—trim the soft-baked cookies. Frost them with black-tinted Royal Icing (page 242). When dry, affix a skull candy with a dot of white Royal Icing (page 242). Then outline the cookie edges using the Decorating Icing piped from a decorating bag fitted with a #1S tip.

To purchase the skull candies as well as the umbrella cookie cutter, visit chandlerscakeandcandy.com.

fruit face

Carve jack-o'-lantern faces out of dried apricots and center them on the cookies, using a dot of Royal Icing (page 242) to make them stay put.

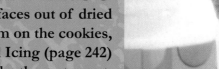

mush for brains

Spread a layer of melted milk-chocolate chips (see "How to Melt Chocolate," page 242) over soft-baked cookies. Before it cools, cover the chocolate with mini-marshmallows in a pattern reminiscent of the two sides of a human brain. If desired, toast the marshmallows using a kitchen torch or by placing the cookies under the broiler for a few moments.

TOXIC assets

Pile up some hazardous-looking cookies topped with green-tinted Easy Icing (page 242) or white cake frosting from the grocery store. Crumbled barley candy or hard candies add a crystalline touch.

STAR POWER

For a super simple cookie sandwich, cut star shapes out of half a package of soft-baked cookies using a cutter or a sharp knife. Melt orange and yellow candy coating, such as Wilton's Candy Melts® which is similar to meltable white chocolate (see "How to Melt Chocolate, page 242). Spread it on a whole cookie, and then top with a cutout cookie.

a LOT ON YOUR PLATE

On a flat circular platter, place cookies edge to edge. Fill in the spaces with raw sugar. Place a jack-o'-lantern stencil from the craft store—or a pattern cut out of wax paper—on top. Fill a sieve with powdered sugar that has been tinted with orange food color pigment, and dust the cookies liberally. Remove the stencil to reveal the pattern.

fresh and wormy

For a tantalizingly icky treat, weave gummy worms through cookies dusted with "dirt," which is really black sanding sugar used for decorating cookies. Use a plastic drinking straw to punch the holes.

To order these realistic brown gummy earth worms, visit candywarehouse.com.

nice and fangy

Give loved ones the giggles with cookies featuring silly Count Dracula faces. Mold white ready-to-use fondant from a craft or cake-decorating store into fang shapes. Add the fangs and candy eyes to the cookies using brown-tinted Royal Icing (page 242) piped from a decorating bag fitted with a #1S tip. For the widow's peak, roll black fondant triangles in black sanding sugar and attach to the cookie with Royal Icing.

creepy cupcakes

Who doesn't love a cupcake? Even the fastidious among us embrace the frosting mustache that comes from sinking our teeth into such a sweet little treat. Save time making these clever morsels by using cake mixes and frostings from the grocery store. Invest in a decorating bag and specialized tips from a craft or specialty foods store to help you accomplish professional details. Then follow these recipes for decorating fun.

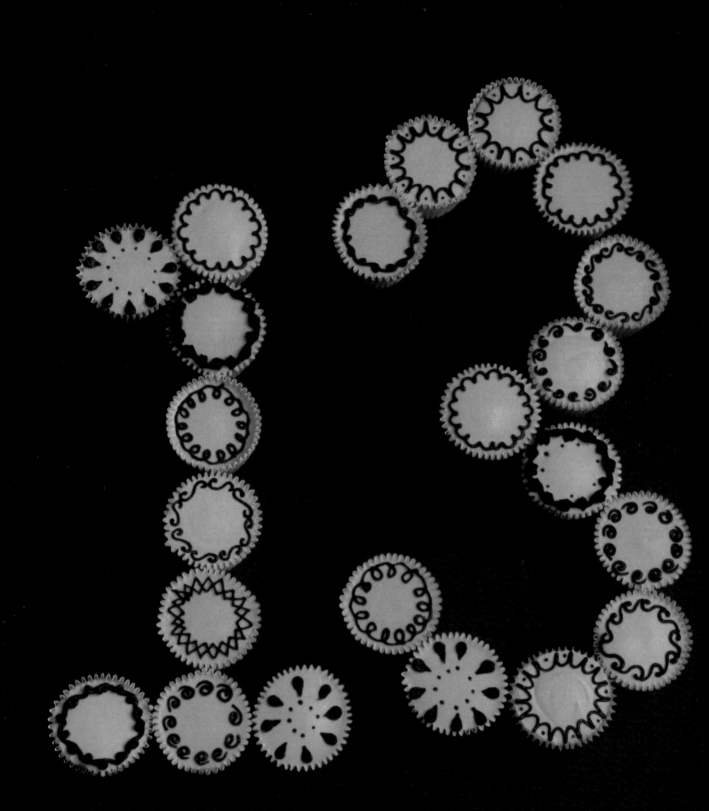

a bite of orange

Array decorated cupcakes in the shape of ominous number 13. Start with a yellow cake mix of your choice. Use a small cookie scoop—similar to an ice cream scoop—to dole out the batter, or fill the liners only half full. Bake according to directions. While the cupcakes cool, mix white frosting with orange gel food coloring to get the desired hue. Warm it in the microwave on 50-percent power setting for one minute to soften the frosting. Drizzle the frosting on the cupcakes until it is level with the top of the wrappers. When the frosting is cool and set, add details using black-tinted Royal Icing (see page 242) piped from a decorating bag fitted with a #1S tip.

eating machine

Use your imagination to design a robot for the top of a trio of cupcakes. Top baked and cooled cupcakes with circles of ready-to-use orange fondant. On a separate baking mat or cutting board, roll out black fondant and cut squares for the robot body parts. Also cut pieces of red fondant for hands, and roll thin lines and small balls for other features. Use white nonpareils or dots of store-bought white Royal Icing (page 242), along with red fondant specks, for the eyes.

garden ghoul

Create a maniacal scarecrow out of a platter full of cupcakes. Arrange about 24 cupcakes into the shape of a scarecrow head on a large platter. You'll need about six cups Easy Icing (page 242). Tint the frosting using gel food colors in brown, red, black, and orange. To make the face, use a little brown gel food color to tint the frosting tan, then spread it over the cupcakes. Press a clean tea towel lightly into the frosting to create texture similar to burlap. Fill decorating bags with frosting and, using a variety of specialty tips, cover the cupcakes with the features of the scarecrow. For the stitched mouth, pipe black frosting using a decorating bag fitted with a #4 tip. For the neck, roll ready-to-use fondant into two thick ropes and twist together. Crushed Shredded Wheat® cereal is edible "straw."

scaredy cat

Set out a tray of cupcakes decorated together to create a large cat face. You could opt to use black frosting to make the kitty more sinister. Start with 22 to 24 cupcakes, baked and cooled. Arrange them on a large round platter as shown. Fill a decorating bag fitted with a #199 tip with Easy Icing (page 242) that has been tinted orange. Squeeze small rosettes all over the tops of the cupcakes to fill in the face. For the tiger stripes, refill the decorating bag with some icing tinted with brown food gel and add triangles to the top and sides of the face. For the cat's features, unroll ready-to-use fondant in orange, green, black, and brown. Cut the shapes and lay them on the frosting. Finally, add black licorice rope whiskers.

To purchase ready-to-use fondant, visit sugarcraft.com, wilton.com, or another site that specializes in baking supplies (see Resources, page 256).

ice screams

Combine cake and ice cream in one handy dessert. Bake a batch of yellow-cake-mix cupcakes in a greased mini-cupcake pan. Fill sugar cones with chocolate ice cream, leaving the top half inch unfilled. Insert cooled cupcakes into the cones. Anchor the cones in an old test-tube tray or a deep roasting pan filled with dried beans. For the frosting, tint white cake frosting orange and purple using gel food color. Microwave it at a 50 percent power setting for 1 minute until it's smooth and creamy. Spread on the cupcakes, then sprinkle with orange and black nonpareils.

vampire snacks

Frost baked and cooled cupcakes with white cake frosting. For the bat motifs, follow the template on page 244 using black gel icing from the grocery or craft store. Poke some extra fun into bat-decorated cupcakes by adding bite marks: Use a toothpick to make two holes and drizzle red gel icing inside.

candy-coated dreams

1   18.25-ounce package red velvet cake mix
1   16-ounce container cream cheese frosting
1   12-ounce package orange or green candy coating
32 ounces milk-chocolate chips
12 large gumdrops
Icing candies shaped like bones
12 flexible silicone baking cups for cupcakes
12 bamboo skewers

1. Bake cake mix in a 9 × 13-inch pan according to package directions. When cool, crumble the cake into a large mixing bowl. Stir in the package of frosting and mix until well combined.

2. Set out baking cups. Melt colored candy coating according to package directions. Using a firm pastry brush or small spatula, paint the insides of the cups with melted candy coating. Allow to cool and set. Remove candy-coated cups from silicone molds.

3. Gently fill cups with cake-and-frosting mixture, mounding the top slightly.

4. Melt chocolate chips (see "How to Melt Chocolate," page 242). Pour melted chocolate over cupcakes. Let cool and set.

5. To turn a cupcake into a lollipop, spread a dab of melted candy coating on the bottom of the cupcake. Invert the gumdrop and press it against the bottom of the candy coating. When affixed, insert a bamboo skewer into the gumdrop.

6. Hand out to your guests, or anchor the skewers in a wide vase filled with orange and black candies, such as M&M's.®

Makes 12 cupcakes

Silicone baking cups and candy coating, such as CandyMelts,® are available at wilton.com and other baking and craft stores (see Resources, page 256).

To order bone-shaped candies, visit chandlerscakeandcandy.com.

EDIBLE WEB

Cast a sugary web that's sure to ensnare guests. Bake and cool 24 cupcakes in any flavor you desire. Arrange 16 of them in a large circle on a platter. Space the remaining eight cupcakes around the outside, as shown. Tint two packages of white cake frosting with black food color gel, reserving one cup of white frosting. Spread the frosting smoothly across the cupcakes, forming an eight-pointed web shape. Dust the frosting with purple edible glitter (from the cake-decorating aisle of the craft store). Finally, fill a decorating bag fitted with a #5 tip with the white frosting. Pipe lines across the cupcakes to form the web. Add plastic spiders for a creepy effect.

one-eyed monsters

1 18.25-ounce package lemon cake mix
2 16-ounce containers white frosting
Yellow and green food color
Yellow and green ready-to-use fondant
Candy icing eyes
Paper cupcake wrappers

Candy toppings

Sour apple Laffy Taffy®
Lemon WarHeads®
Sour apple Trolli-O's®
Yellow M&M's® MINIS®
Green apple licorice laces

1. Bake cupcakes according to manufacturer's directions and let cool.

2. Tint cake frosting yellow and green. Frost cupcakes.

3. Play with your food! Roll Laffy Taffy into worm bodies or tentacles. Trim licorice laces into spiky "hair." Mold fondant into a monster mouth or nostril shapes. Add candy icing eyes to WarHeads using a dot of frosting as glue. Put M&M's spots on the worm body using frosting to adhere.

Makes about 24 cupcakes

All of these candies can be purchased online from candywarehouse.com.

Get slimed

1   3-ounce package lemon- or lime-flavored Jell-O® gelatin
4   ounces Knox® unflavored gelatin
6   gummy worms
6   flexible silicone baking cups
6   teacups with round bottoms

1. Combine flavored and unflavored gelatin packages in a mixing bowl with a pour spout. Pour in 1½ cups boiling water. Stir until dissolved completely, about 3 minutes.

2. Fill silicone baking cups. Pour remaining liquid into teacups, filling only a half inch. (This will make domes for the cupcakes.)

3. Refrigerate for 4 hours until set. To remove the gelatin from baking cups and teacups, immerse the bottom of cups in a bowl of warm water for a few seconds. Turn over cups and gently pry cupcakes out.

4. Invert domes on top of cupcakes. Lay gummy worms on top.

Makes 6 cupcakes

GOOD FOR YOU GOODIES

Turn kids on to healthy Halloween treats with these devilishly clever packaging ideas. Make snack-size treats from larger quantity packages—saving on cost is an added bonus. You can download all of our labels at matthewmeadstyle.com, or, of course, make your own.

monster bites

Mix up a batch of leftover Frankenstein parts using honey-roasted peanuts (the nuts), oat-ring cereal (the bolts), and any other trail mix ingredient, such as milk-chocolate chips. Fill cellophane or plastic bags with the mix and tuck them into empty quart-size paint cans from a home center or craft store. Affix labels with double-stick tape.

produced on a machine with rusty parts and leaky

doctor frankenstein's

nuts & bolts

pieces and parts from monsters that just didn't work out

crunchy bits of vermin in every bite

produced on a machine with rusty parts and leaky

doctor frankenstein's

nuts & bolts

pieces and parts from monsters that just didn't work out

crunchy bits of vermin in every bit

produced on a machine with rusty parts and leaky lubricant

doctor frankenstein's

nuts & bolts

pieces and parts from monsters that just didn't work out

crunchy bits of vermin in every bite.

DARKLY DELECTABLE

Make ordinary banana chips and dried cranberries revoltingly attractive by selling them as packages of animal organs. Put the combo into plastic snack bags or cellophane bags from the craft store and staple or tape on the label.

shriveled red rats eyes **AND SLIVERED BAT BRAIN**

A CHEWY AND CRUNCHY SNACK WITH HORRIBLE ODOR AND FOUL AFTERTASTE.

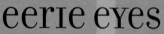

eerie eyes

Turn yogurt-covered almonds, malted-milk balls, and raisins into eyeballs using black food-safe markers from the cake-decorating aisle of the craft store (see *Resources,* page 256). Fill and label repurposed tube-shaped candy containers.

malted eyeballs PICKLED IN YOGURT

milky malted eyeballs PICKLED IN YOGURT

ed eyeballs N YOGURT

blood Curdled
ADAM'S APPLE SAUCE
TAKE A BITE
EXP. FRIDAY 13 2020

PULPY DELIGHT

Make party guests squeal by suggesting this innocent berry-flavored applesauce is for the bloodthirsty among them. We used single-serving natural applesauce containers and added labels onto the foil lids with double-stick tape.

YUCKY YUMMIES

Encourage kids to eat these boogers—really clear bags of golden raisins with clever labels taped to the top. Embellish with an orange ribbon if desired.

troll boogers
GOLDEN, CHEWY, TASTY BITES
troll boogers
GOLDEN, CHEWY, TASTY BITES
LISTEN
GOLDEN,
TASTY,
MINED BY HAND.
SOMETIMES
CRUNCHY
WITH
GROUND UP
SAND.

shriveled treats

Hand out boxes of raisins disguised as ingredients in a witch's brew to wee trick-or-treaters. Print the labels on bright papers and tape them to the boxes.

death wormed over

Give craft-store coffins a personal touch with paint and silly labels. Sesame sticks inside are reminiscent of maggots. Paint the coffins with black acrylic paint, glue on the labels with spray-adhesive, then insert bags of treats.

To order these 6-inch-long wooden coffins, go to michaels.com.

cookie monsters

Lurking in your local grocery store are hordes of packaged cookies that can quickly be turned into the sweetest sinister spooks. We enhanced these with a little icing, food markers, cutouts, and candies—and a lot of imagination.

LOST SOULS

Melt 6 ounces white-chocolate chips; transfer to a 1-gallon plastic food-storage bag. Allow the chocolate to settle in one corner; then squeeze the air out and seal the bag. Cut a ⅛-inch piece from the corner (you can cut more later if the hole is too small; if the hole is too large, it will be hard to control the design). Draw a mournful face onto each cookie. Work quickly—if the chocolate gets too cool, it will be hard to squeeze. Use a paint marker or dry-transfer letters to write "Lost Souls" on the jar.

DING-a-LING SPIDER

80 dark-chocolate biscuit sticks (we used
    Pocky®), plain ends broken off
10 chocolate-covered cream-filled cakes
    (we used Ring Dings®)

2   ounces (2 squares) semisweet
    baking chocolate, melted
5   miniature marshmallows
10 pairs candy eyes

1. Dip the broken end of a biscuit stick into melted chocolate and insert it near
the top of a cake; repeat to give each spider eight legs.

2. Using a paring knife or small shears, cut each miniature marshmallow into
four small triangles for the spider's teeth. Add teeth and candy eyes as shown,
affixing each with a dab of melted chocolate applied with a toothpick.

To order Pocky, visit amazon.com.

ICY STARES

Make these quick-as-a-wink. You can even put your kids in charge of this project. Start with iced oatmeal cookies (we used Archway® cookies) and draw eyes on them with food markers, which can be found in a cake-decorating shop. We used black and yellow markers, but your eyes can be as colorful as you like.

BISCOTTI VIPERS

Start with 12 purchased biscotti. Melt 8 ounces white baking chocolate; transfer to a 1-gallon plastic food-storage bag. Snip ⅛-inch from one corner of the bag. Squeeze serpent shapes onto the biscotti and let the chocolate harden. Melt four ounces semisweet chocolate and transfer to a small plastic food-storage bag. Snip ¹⁄₁₆-inch from one corner and pipe a pattern of stripes or dots onto each serpent. Let chocolate harden before serving.

BLACK MAGIC DRAGON

This fire-breathing monster makes a whimsical centerpiece for a dessert buffet.

24 chocolate cake sandwich cookies (we used Oreo® Cakesters)
½   cup ready-to-use white fondant
2   large candy eyes (Buy more candy eyes if you want to make
     dragon heads only, as shown on page 71.)
Green and orange food color

1. Arrange as many cookies as fit in an olive dish as shown (or stack them in pairs to make dragon heads). Cut the remainder in half.

2. Tint about ⅓ cup fondant green and the rest orange. Roll out the green fondant to ⅛-inch thickness and cut three to four "spines" for each half cookie; insert the spines into the half-cookies and arrange as shown.

3. Cut two green rounds slightly larger than the candy eyes. Affix the eyes to the green rounds with a dampened finger, then attach the rounds to the dragon head.

4. Roll out the orange fondant and cut a long, skinny, forked tongue; use a toothpick to insert it.

masked scholars

Who doesn't love those chocolate schoolboy biscuits? Start with a package of *Le Petit Ecolier*® biscuits in dark chocolate and milk chocolate. To dress the boys up, mix a batch of Royal Icing (page 242). Use orange, green, and black gel food color to tint 1½ cups of the icing orange, 1 tablespoon green, and 1 tablespoon black; leave the rest white. Using decorating bags fitted with #1S tips, pipe the orange and white icings onto the cookies as shown. Draw eyes in the mask with a toothpick dipped in the black icing. Draw jack-o'-lantern faces with the black icing; draw pumpkin stems with a toothpick dipped in the green icing.

BLack cat cookies

You'll need black card stock, yellow acrylic paint, a few tubes of piping gel, chocolate-covered marshmallow-topped cookies (such as Mallomars® or Whippets™), toothpicks, and black and orange nonpareils. Copy or scan and print the cat template on page 244. For each cat, trace the template onto card stock and use a craft knife to cut it out. Paint the eyes, nose, and whiskers on one side. Tape a toothpick to the back, leaving 1 inch extending below the bottom of the card stock. Spread the top of a cookie with piping gel and sprinkle with nonpareils. Gently push the cat cutout into the cookie.

POP STARS

Elevate good old popcorn into a real crowd pleaser with these easy recipes. There's something to satisfy every palate—sweet, savory, or both.

CRUNCHY CARAMEL CORN

5–6 quarts of plain popped popcorn
1   cup butter
2   cups brown sugar
½   cup light corn syrup
1   teaspoon salt
½   teaspoon baking soda
1   teaspoon vanilla

1. Preheat oven to 250°F. Spray the inside of a brown paper grocery bag with cooking spray and fill with popcorn.

2. In a medium sauté pan, melt the butter. Stir in brown sugar, corn syrup, and salt. Bring to a boil, stirring constantly. Boil without stirring for 4 minutes, then remove from heat and add baking soda and vanilla. Stir well.

3. Pour caramel sauce over the popcorn in the paper bag. Fold over the top of the bag and shake to coat. Divide the mixture and place onto two parchment-paper-lined cookie sheets.

4. Bake for an hour, stirring every 15 minutes. Remove from oven and allow popcorn to cool completely.

Makes about 11 cups

FINGER LICKING

In a large mixing bowl, combine Crunchy Caramel Corn with chocolate-covered peanut-butter candies.

GHOSTLY GOOD

Give the Crunchy Caramel Corn a Halloween twist by tossing in
ghost candies (from the cookie-decorating section of the craft
store). While the caramel corn is still warm from the oven, sprinkle
in the ghost candies so they stick to bite-size clumps.

LUCY THU

ZESTY BLEND

Create a sweet-and-salty snack mix by drizzling a sugar glaze over cayenne-dusted popcorn and peanuts.

½   cup kernels (yields about 12 cups popped plain popcorn)
1   cup salted peanuts
½   cup unsalted butter
1   cup sugar
¼   cup light corn syrup
½   teaspoon coarse salt
¼   teaspoon cayenne pepper

1. Preheat oven to 250°F.

2. If using kernels, pop on the stovetop or in an air-popper.

3. Combine popped popcorn and peanuts in a large bowl and set aside.

4. Combine butter, sugar, and corn syrup in a medium saucepan over medium heat. Cook, stirring occasionally until sugar has dissolved. Increase heat to medium-high and cook, without stirring, until golden brown, about 5 minutes, swirling pot occasionally.

5. Remove mixture from heat and quickly stir in salt and cayenne. Immediately pour over popcorn mixture and stir to incorporate.

6. Divide popcorn mixture evenly between two parchment-paper-lined baking sheets.

7. Bake 20 minutes, stirring occasionally.

8. Let cool completely before breaking apart into clusters. Then store in resealable plastic bags or air-tight containers.

Makes about 13 cups

all bark and bite

Make melt-in-your-mouth bark by adding the Crunchy Caramel Corn (page 80) to melted milk chocolate.

32 ounces (2 bags) milk chocolate chips
2   cups Crunchy Caramel Corn (page 80)
1   cup mixed nuts
12 sugar icing bones
12 sugar icing pumpkins

1. Put chips in a medium glass mixing bowl and microwave on medium power for 1 minute. Stir, then heat 30 seconds more at medium power. Repeat every 30 seconds until chocolate is mostly melted.

2. Remove chocolate from microwave, stir thoroughly again (the chips will completely melt at this point).

3. On a parchment-paper-lined baking sheet, spread the chocolate into an even layer.

4. Press Crunchy Caramel Corn, nuts, and icing decorations into the chocolate before it hardens. Let cool for at least 2 hours. Break into pieces, which you can package in cellophane gift bags or store in air-tight containers.

To order these candies, visit chandlerscakeandcandy.com.

sugar and spice

Combine plain popcorn with cinnamon graham cracker cereal, chocolate candies, and chewy dates and raisins for a delectable mix.

10 cups popped popcorn
1   cup raisins
2   cups cinnamon-flavored graham cracker cereal
1½ cups miniature marshmallows
1   cup chopped dried dates
¼   cup melted butter
¼   cup firmly packed light brown sugar
2   teaspoons ground cinnamon
¼   teaspoon ground ginger
½   teaspoon ground nutmeg

1. Preheat oven to 250°F.

2. Combine popcorn, raisins, cereal, marshmallows, and dates in a large roasting pan; stir well to combine.

3. Combine remaining ingredients in a small bowl. Pour into popcorn mixture and stir to combine.

4. Bake for 20 minutes, stirring once after 10 minutes.

5. Let mixture cool, then store in resealable plastic bags or air-tight containers.

Makes 12 to 14 cups

great Balls

Roll up some kid pleasers with sweetly simple popcorn balls. Display them on a candelabra for a dramatic party centerpiece, or package the treats to give away.

¾ cup light corn syrup
¼ cup margarine
2 teaspoons cold water
2½ cups confectioners' sugar
1 cup miniature marshmallows
5 quarts plain popped popcorn
1 tablespoon vegetable shortening or cooking spray

1. In a saucepan over medium heat, combine the corn syrup, margarine, cold water, confectioners' sugar, and marshmallows. Heat and stir the mixture until it comes to a boil.

2. Remove from heat and carefully pour the hot mixture over the popcorn in a large mixing bowl. Stir thoroughly to coat each kernel.

3. Grease hands with vegetable shortening or cooking spray and quickly shape the coated popcorn into balls before it cools and hardens.

4. Wrap with plastic wrap and store at room temperature.

Makes about 15 popcorn balls

SPINE CHILLERS

If you need a (short) break from Halloween candy, ice cream is the perfect sweet substitute! Add toppings, cookies, and pumpkin faces—or even flapping paper bat wings—for treats that will chill and thrill.

candy corn freeze

White, orange, and yellow stripes are one of the unofficial symbols of Halloween. This candy-corn inspired ice cream parfait is the perfect ending to any autumn party.

1   quart orange sherbet
1   half-gallon vanilla ice cream
3   disposable decorating bags
9   clear 10-ounce glasses
Yellow paste or gel food color
Orange nonpareils, for garnish

1. Let the sherbet and ice cream sit at room temperature until softened, about 15 minutes. Transfer the sherbet to a decorating bag. Transfer 4 cups of the ice cream to another decorating bag. Place them in the freezer.

2. Adding a few drops at a time, mix some yellow food color into the remaining ice cream. Transfer the yellow ice cream to the third decorating bag. Pipe some yellow ice cream into the bottom third of each glass. Put the glasses in the freezer.

3. Remove the decorating bag with sherbet from the freezer to soften. When it is soft enough to pipe, remove the glasses from the freezer and pipe an even layer of sherbet into each. Return the glasses to the freezer.

4. Remove the decorating bag with the white ice cream from the freezer to soften, and pipe it into each glass. Return the glasses to the freezer. Remove them about 15 minutes before serving. Just before serving, sprinkle each parfait with nonpareils.

Makes 9 servings

JACK-O'-SHERBET

Let devouring this smiley pumpkin-face treat be a group activity or present it with a flourish and then spoon it into individual bowls. Start with 1 quart of orange sherbet in a transparent tub. Remove the lid. Draw a jack-o'-lantern face onto the top with quick-to-freeze chocolate topping (we used Magic Shell®). If you're making more than one, a bat or witch's face design would be fun too. Serve with classic wooden ice cream spoons.

OCTOBER PARFAIT

For four parfaits, you'll need 1 quart of dark chocolate ice cream, 1 pint of orange sherbet, one 8-ounce container of nondairy whipped topping, about 1 cup chocolate cookie crumbs (we crushed 20 chocolate wafer cookies to make about 1 cup of crumbs), and ¼ cup shelled peanuts. Place a scoop of ice cream in the bottom of each parfait glass. Add a scoop of sherbet. Sprinkle on 2 tablespoons cookie crumbs. Add a small scoop of ice cream and then ⅓ cup whipped topping. Top with 1 tablespoon cookie crumbs and a tablespoon peanuts. Yum!

screamwiches

Make a batch of Royal Icing (page 242); use gel or paste food color to tint half of it orange. Put each color in a decorating bag fitted with a #1 or #2 tip. Pipe designs on the tops of 12 chocolate wafer cookies (we used Famous® Chocolate Wafers) and let them dry completely. Let 1 quart of orange sherbet soften slightly, then sandwich scoops between pairs of cookies, placing the decorated ones on top. Freeze in a single layer on a baking sheet until serving.

BATTY BOMBE

Here's a way to end your party with a memorable flap. You'll need a dome-shape ice cream cake with dark chocolate frosting, a bag of small candies (such as Skittles® Chocolate Mix), two large candy eyes, one 8½ × 11-inch piece each black and orange card stock, two wooden skewers, and double-stick tape.

Copy or scan and print the bat wing pattern on page 246 (or create your own bat wings). Cut two small black wings, two large black wings, and two large orange wings from the card stock. Layer and tape them together as shown in the photo. Also cut a 1½-inch skinny orange triangle to be the bat's tongue. Cut the skewers to 6 inches long. Place the cake on a plate. Gently press the candy eyes and the tongue into the frosting as shown. Bend the bat wings, angle each against the cake, and support them from underneath with a skewer (pointed end inserted into the cake). Scatter the candies around the base.

freaky fudge POPS

Line a baking sheet or shallow pan with parchment paper (make sure it will fit in your freezer first). Unwrap chocolate fudge ice cream bars and arrange them on the baking sheet. Let sit until slightly softened, 3 to 5 minutes. Lightly press one or more pairs of candy eyes onto each bar. Sprinkle with orange and yellow nonpareils. Place in the freezer until ready to serve.

SILLY CHILLY STICKS

Candy-coated ice cream bars are even more fun to eat when embellished with funny Halloween figures. (Use a variety of bars if you like; we used M&M's® Ice Cream Treats and Dove® Ice Cream Bars.) Affix a candy decoration to each ice cream bar with a dot of ready-made icing or melted chocolate. Freeze until serving.

To order the decorations shown, visit chandlerscakeandcandy.com.

creepy, clever crafts

Creative projects using pumpkins, gourds, and simple materials from the craft store

PUMPKINS PERSONIFIED

Move beyond the plain old pumpkins to make clever jacks out of painted walnuts and acorns, paper lanterns, or even dog toys. You're guaranteed to get chuckles from friends and family who come face-to-face with these happy hobgoblins. Some can be quickly assembled just for this year's festivities, and others will become part of your annual decorating scheme.

JUICED UP

Raid the fruit bowl for a trio of oranges to decorate like a snowman. Stack small oranges or clementines on a bamboo skewer and place in a teacup or small ramekin to keep them from wobbling. Use black construction paper to form a witch's hat and facial features, and secure with dots of hot glue. Poke in twigs for arms.

NUT CASES

Paint the shells of whole walnuts and pecans to make these adorable little guys. Brush on orange acrylic paint and, when dry, use a fine-tip permanent marker to draw on features. Form stems from brown modeling clay, and stick to the top. Fill a bowl with the wee jacks or stand them up on a bookcase, using a small bit of modeling clay or Tacky Wax® to secure the bottoms.

LAMP-O'-LANTERN

With an ornate Victorian sconce or candelabra, you can give a paper lantern new sophistication. Or place paper lanterns (with features cut from scrapbook paper and adhered with craft glue) over the bulbs of your chandelier. Be careful not to let the paper come into contact with the hot bulbs.

To purchase this lantern visit pearlriver.com.

take the stand

Give a jack-o'-lantern the full-body treatment
by displaying it on a vintage plant stand. An
enamel cake dome, placed rakishly off-kilter,
animates the white pumpkin with a painted
face. Bowls of candy are for doorbell ringers,
but they also have the look of hands. Search
for similar tiered stands (this one probably
dates to the 1970s) at garage sales and
thrift stores; any style will do as long as the
pumpkin sits at the top.

DISAPPEARING ACT

Conjure a magical scene that suggests someone has been charmed into a pumpkin. Hot-glue a mask on an heirloom pumpkin, seat it in a chair, then dangle witch stockings over the back.

IN THE CAN

Turn a small trash can or compost bin into a pumpkin with glossy orange spray paint (formulated for metal) and a festive expression. For a temporary decoration, cut features out of black duct tape or masking tape and stick on. You could also paint the features using black spray paint and a stencil from the craft store.

FETCH FRIEND

Personalize a hard rubber chew toy for your best friend—naughty or nice—with humorous jack-o'-lantern features added in permanent black marker.

To purchase this Bad Cuz Rubber Walking Ball from JW Pet Company, visit amazon.com.

BOTTLE neck

Affix a cheery smirk on a large colorful lollipop, then plop the character in a colorful bottle with cotton spiderwebs snaking out. Cut the features out of ready-to-use fondant rolled very thin. Use icing gel from the craft store to affix the features.

For large swirl lollipops in Halloween colors, visit candywarehouse.com.

107

Grocery Ghouls

Pumpkin carving is just the beginning of the fun to be had with autumn's bounty of produce. If you can cut a notch with a paring knife, you can put a ghoulish face on fresh produce; harmless eggplants, corn on the cob, or carrots are creepy when they fix you with a sinister stare. Or transform potatoes into crawly spiders, and squash into eerie grinning candleholders. The produce department will never look the same!

Arachnophobia

JACK OH! LANTERN

Pumpkins often have the coolest stems. When you shop for a pumpkin to carve, turn it on its side to see what sort of nose the stem will make—surprised, spooky, snide, or silly—then let the stem guide the style of the other features.

1. Turn the pumpkin on its side. With a kitchen knife, cut a hole in the bottom, making it no larger than needed for you to scoop out the insides. If you are able to get it out in one piece, set the cutout aside to use as a plug later.

2. Clean out the pumpkin interior.

3. Using the stem as the nose, draw eyes, a mouth, and any other facial features you wish on the pumpkin.

4. Using a paring knife or carving tool, cut away the outer rind in each eye; leave the golden flesh as shown. Cut out the mouth. If you've drawn other features, cut them out partially or completely as you wish.

5. Break a toothpick in half. Insert one half in each eye where you want the pupil to be; leave about ⅜ inch extending. Cut a red grape in half crosswise. Place each half, cut-side down, onto the toothpick.

corn-on-the-cob SPIES

Fresh corn with an unflinching black-eyed pea gaze will unnerve your friends. Steam the ears first if you're serving for dinner.

For each cob, peel away half the husk. Choose two kernels for the eye location, then slit each one with a paring knife and insert a black-eyed pea. Arrange in a napkin-lined bowl or basket.

GHOULISH GRIN candleholders

Unusual or exotic squash and gourds, especially ones with toothless grins like these chayote squash, give you a head start on the character for veggie candleholders.

Once you've found a squash or gourd with the right "mouth," carve a spot for a tea light with a paring knife or grapefruit spoon. Cut a small cavity for each eye with a paring knife and insert black-eyed peas, lentils, or other dried legumes to make bleary eyes.

tapered terrors

Skinny carrots with quirky shapes and intense black-eyed pea eyes only look like creepy orange candles, and any visitor will be sure to give them a second glance. Wash and peel the carrots first if you think your guests will want to nibble. With a paring knife, cut two little notches where you want the eyes to be and firmly press the peas into them.

spider spuds

Make a gang of these for a hair-raising event. We used small purple potatoes, but spuds of various shapes and colors will make a truly terrifying infestation.

If you wish, rub the potato with cooking oil to give it a sheen. Wipe off any excess oil before continuing. With a paring knife, cut two small cavities at one end of each potato where you want the eyes to be; press a black-eyed pea into each.

For the legs, cut six 3-inch-long pieces of pussy willow or other flexible twig. Gently bend a joint to form each leg. With a skewer, poke three holes along each side of the potato; insert a leg in each.

an eye for EGGPLANT

With their long stems and soft, funny caps, Thai eggplants have natural personalities, which you can enhance by adding acrylic paint eyes.

These unusual veggies come from the exotic produce section in a grocery store or specialty food market. Use small paintbrushes or paint pens to give each eggplant a disconcerting stare. Tape or tie one end of a length of thin, stiff cord (about 8 inches long) to a foil-wrapped candy, then tie the other end around the eggplant stem.

113

JOLLY JACKS

Make the most of your decorating dollar by featuring inexpensive, unfinished wood pumpkin cutouts that you embellish yourself. Here are a dozen different looks for these happy fellows, which cost about $2 a piece at craft stores. Make as many as you like, then hang them as window decorations, incorporate them in a mantel arrangement, or even tape them on the garage door to greet trick-or-treaters on the special night.

To buy these 10-inch wooden pumpkin cutouts, go to your local Michaels store (visit michaels.com for a store locator).

ribbon winner

Stretch spunky ribbons across an orange-painted cutout, weaving strips over and under for interest. Attach the ribbon edges to the back using hot glue.

aLL THaT jazz

To make this sparkly gem, first paint the cutout white with acrylic paint. When dry, brush on white craft glue. Once the glue gets tacky, press in clear orange beads to cover.

THE COWBOY WAY

Cover the face of the cutout with spray adhesive in a well-ventilated area. While the glue is tacky, place a bandana on the cutout, centering the design on the eyes. Smooth the bandana in place and allow the glue to dry. Cut small slits in the eye, nose, and mouth openings using an X-Acto knife, and use scissors to trim off excess material, leaving ½-inch around the perimeter. Wrap any extra bandana to the back of the cutout and hot-glue in place.

WRAP ME UP

Brush on a light coat of decoupage medium such as Mod Podge® to cover the pumpkin cutout. Smooth on a piece of graphic wrapping paper. Trim it to fit the cutout, and apply a topcoat of decoupage medium to protect the surface.

117

FRESH AS A DAISY

Pick some festive paper posies from the scrapbooking aisle of the craft store. You could also use silk flowers. Hot-glue the petals to an orange-painted cutout. For the centers, use beads or roll balls out of yellow modeling clay and hot-glue in place.

GET IT ON TAPE

Tear strips of orange and yellow masking tape, which is available in a variety of shades from craft and office-supply stores, to decorate an orange-painted cutout.

GIVE IT SOME BLING

For sparkle and shine, coat the
entire face of the cutout with
orange and black glitter from the
craft store. Brush on white craft glue
edge to edge, and, when tacky, sprinkle
on the orange glitter. If desired, once the
glue is dry you can go back over the edges
with more glue and add a black glitter outline.
When dry, pick up the cutout and shake off

CANDY-COATED

For a deliciously creative project, hot-glue orange chocolate-covered candies on a black-painted pumpkin. (Keep this one out of reach to avoid tempting small children or pets.)

GOING BUGGY

Glue on children's plastic toys to give this pumpkin 3-D interest. Paint the cutout with black acrylic paint, then use hot glue to secure the bugs and a small plastic magnifying glass.

OUT-STAMPING DESIGN

On a white-painted cutout, create a random design using rubber stamps and black ink. You could use any motif, from friendly flowers to spooky skulls.

CHALKBOARD CHARM

Paint the cutout with chalkboard paint, which can be found in paint stores and craft stores. When dry, sketch a holiday illustration, such as a crow or spider, or add gruesome stitch marks à la Frankenstein.

warm & FUZZY PUMPKINS

Get your creative juices flowing with these frighteningly cute fiber projects. Weave a skein of yarn into the number 13, or sculpt loose wool fibers into felted Halloween favorites, such as spiders and witch hats.

GOING BATTY

Using the pattern on page 247, nail brads into the side of a pumpkin, leaving a small portion of each brad sticking out. Starting at the bat's left shoulder, wrap smooth black yarn around the brads until the outline is complete. (You'll need less than a yard of yarn.) Wrap the end tightly around the last brad, secure with a drop of hot glue, and clip any excess yarn. Add eyes and fangs with black acrylic craft paint.

GOTCHa!

Snare a pumpkin in a black yarn web. Wrap it with shaggy chenille yarn, which can be found in most craft or fabric stores, or use smooth yarn. To start and finish the wrapping, secure the loose ends with a dot of hot glue.

aLL wrappeD up

Inspired by Charlie Brown's sweater in *It's the Great Pumpkin, Charlie Brown*, this argyle pattern suits a big orange pumpkin. Nail brads into rows, adjusting the intervals as necessary to fit your particular squash. Then wrap smooth and shaggy black yarns around them.

GET STARTED
NEEDLE FELTING

Long popular with needleworkers and knitters, felting is catching on as a craft anyone can do. That's because it involves a simple technique, lends itself to any creative idea you might have, and can be accomplished in little time. See page 146 for more about the basic felting technique, then apply what you learn to these fun projects.

Purchase packages of wool roving, which looks a little like cotton candy. You'll need orange, black, and white roving.

Buy the tools: a single needle for felting small details, such as the spider's eyeball, and a multineedle tool for felting large pieces, such as the witch's hat.

Protect your work surface with a dense foam pad (at least 3 inches thick) or a bristle pad, which looks like an overturned scrub brush. Either one will absorb the punches of the sharp felting needles.

snakes alive!

Slithering to a pumpkin near you, this snake is a quick felting project. Measure around your pumpkin and cut out a long-enough reptile shape from black felt or wool fabric. Lay it on your work pad, and then use felting needles to edge it with shaggy chenille yarn. Attach a tongue and felted eyeballs in the same manner. Wrap the snake around the pumpkin and attach with common pins.

friendly spider

Fashion this adorable arachnid out of jet-black roving. Punch a medium-size ball with felting needles to make the flat body. Then felt a smaller ball for the head and eight skinny legs. Join the pieces by overlapping them slightly on your work surface and punching the needles through the overlap to unite the fibers. Felt small white-and-black eyeballs, and join them to the head. When finished, attach the spider to a pie-size pumpkin with straight pins.

WITCH'S BRIM

Cut a pointy hat shape out of black felt or
wool fabric and place it on your work surface.
Edge it with chenille yarn using felting
needles. For the white band, stretch a strip
of white roving across the hat, and felt
it in place with the needles. Sculpt
a buckle out of white and black
roving, and felt them to the hat
as well. Attach the hat to the
pumpkin using straight pins
or needles.

gourd warmer

For a clever tabletop or front-step decoration, embellish a plain stocking cap with a jack-o'-lantern face stitched out of yarn. Snip a small opening at the top of the cap for the gourd stem. A small, child-size hat works best.

someone's watching

Using felting needle (the single needle is best for these small forms), sculpt eyeballs out of black and white roving. Let these examples inspire your own creations. When you have completed a few felted eyeballs, cut holes in a pumpkin and insert them.

net gains

Turn the ancient yarn-weaving art of macramé into a festive Halloween candy holder. Hang the holder from a plant hook or doorknob, suspend a hollowed-out pumpkin (spray-painted black for ghoulish effect) in the seat of the net, and fill with candies.

10 pieces orange yarn, each 36 inches in length
Small nail to secure topknot
Hollowed-out pumpkin
Black acrylic spray paint

1. To form the net, first gather all your lengths of smooth orange yarn in a cluster, and knot them together 5 inches from one end of the bunch (1). Secure the knot under a heavy book or by tacking it to a work surface with tape or a small nail (to make pulling the yarns and knotting them easier).

2. Separating the long loose ends into pairs, tie each pair into a knot 10 inches from the large knot (2).

3. Move down another 4 inches, mate one strand with a strand from a neighboring pair to create a new pair, and knot them together (3).

4. Move down another four inches, reform the original pairs and tie knots. Repeat this process twice more at 4-inch intervals until you have 5 inches of loose yarn remaining (4).

5. Tie all 10 strands together to leave a tassel hanging from the bottom (5).

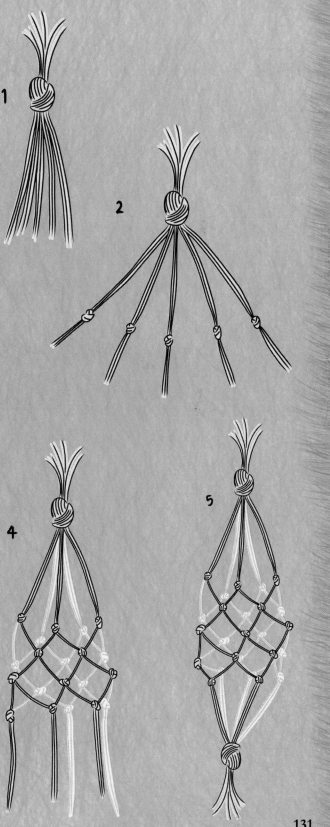

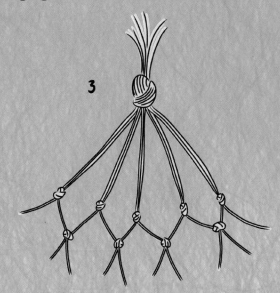

Illustrations: Matt Shay

131

STICKS & STONES

Infinitely malleable, objects from the natural world have the power to transform from ordinary to extraordinary. In the right setting, a three-pronged twig becomes a severed chicken foot and a seashell becomes a brain specimen. By combining your creativity with craft-store tools, such as paint pens and dried moss, you can unearth the spirits within this bounty from the backyard.

THE LAB

Conjure the makings of a mad scientist's laboratory with specimens under plant cloches and a collection of twig "bones." Capture a spiderweb (copied from page 255 or downloaded from matthewmeadstyle.com) and trace over the design with a white gel pen from the craft store. When dry, place it in a photo frame and hang.

IT'S a WRAP

Pair smooth, bark-free twigs with river rocks to create bones. Hot-glue two stones together for each bone tip, then attach the pairs to the sticks with more hot glue. When dry, wrap the bones with strips of white muslin or sheeting. Daub on wet tea to stain the wrappings. Make a label or download this one from matthewmeadstyle.com.

a HEAD aBOVE

For a haunting silhouette, use hot glue to cover a foam wig head with dried moss. This is "reindeer moss," found in the floral aisle of the craft store.

Purchased from amazon.com, this wig head costs less than $5. You can search local beauty-supply or wig stores for similar foam forms.

count mossman
specimen 1890

Discoverd by Lord Treefore
on a fox outing

135

HeaDs UP

Make a papier-mâché skull, purchased from artbeatgifts.com, appear recently unearthed from a grave by painting it with cream acrylic paint. Give it the look of age with a light wash of burnt-sienna pigment from the craft store.

creepy crawly

Dangle a spider on the fridge or magnetic bulletin board and pin it in place with decorated rocks turned into magnets. Download this illustration from matthewmeadstyle.com. Print it on parchment-colored paper. Trace over the shape with white craft glue and dust liberally with black glitter.

SHOCK EFFECT

Select an arrangement of glass canisters, vases, and goblets and fill with the imaginative ingredients of a witch's brew. Create your own labels or download the ones pictured from matthewmeadstyle.com. Then have fun with plastic spiders, cotton webs, seedpods, twigs, and shells.

POUDRE DE SANTÉ

WARLOCK ROOT

USE AFTER MIDNIGHT
ON A RAINY EVE
ARE YOU DULL
A SCARY REPRIEVE

PHARMACIE H DANDOY
TEL 15.88.90

petrified elf feet

161-163 Rue Royale Ste Marie BRUXELLES

PHARMACIE COSMOPOLITE

SCARY DREAMS

take up a collection

Creep out guests with a collection of severed heads—really just peeled and cleverly carved apples in a jar full of white vinegar. Fill in the skull features with black gel icing from the cake-decorating aisle of the craft store.

Door Decor

With a foam wreath as a base, apply natural elements to create a unique decoration. Insert twigs and the stems of lotus seedpods (from the floral aisle of the craft store), using hot glue as necessary to stabilize items. Layer on dried moss, sticks, and grocery-store button mushrooms, which have been sprayed with stone-texture paint from the craft store. Finally, string cotton webs as desired.

139

cast a stone

Paint smooth river rocks with chalkboard paint.
Scatter rocks with Halloween words chalked on
them across the tabletop, in a centerpiece bowl,
or around a guest's setting.

frame UP

Display children's toy bugs in vintage specimen frames or new shadow boxes. Spruce up the frame with a coat of black paint and add a new paper background. Then hot-glue the plastic bugs in place. Or frame a ghostly leaf.

GHOUL BRAIN

SHELL OF AN IDEA

Turn an ordinary sea biscuit—a puffy sea urchin commonly found in souvenir shops and craft stores—into a ghoul brain by coating it with black spray paint. Nestle it in a bed of moss in a glass box.

rocks of ages

Using fine-tip black gel pens, which are scrapbooking tools with intense inks, add skeleton and skull faces to white river rocks. Look for bags of the smooth rocks at craft stores or plant nurseries. Fill a shallow dish with them, or hot-glue magnets to the back and stack them on the fridge.

142

SPOOKY FOLIAGE

Press leaves from neighborhood trees between books for a couple of days, then brush with cream-color acrylic paint. Let dry, then stamp with Halloween icons, or use black acrylic paint to create ghost eyes. The eyeballs are white rocks with gloss-black circles painted on.

SHEEPY HOLLOW

If you've never felted wool before, these adorable Halloween characters offer the perfect excuse to give it a try.

Laughing Ghoul PUMPKIN

Is he a pumpkin, a gremlin, or a sprite who's lost his body? You decide. He's about 6½ inches in diameter. Making him is fun for anyone who has mastered the art of sculpting wool roving; The "Needle Felting Techniques" on page 146 will guide you in adding the stem and facial features that give this guy real personality.

GHOST Garland

Hang a string of these moaning felt ghosts across a doorway or along your mantel. You'll need white felt, a felting needle, a large piece of upholstery foam, white and black wool roving, a length of loosely twisted black yarn, a sewing needle, and white thread.

Copy or scan and print the ghost patterns on page 248, enlarging as desired (ours are about 7½ inches long). Trace the ghosts onto the felt and cut out. (Or cut your own ghosts freehand.) Lay the ghosts one at a time on the foam block, place a small bit of white roving at the end of each arm, and poke it into place with the felting needle. Use tiny bits of black roving to make the eyes and nose, poking each into place with the felting needle. Attach the ghosts to the black yarn with white thread.

The little black-and-white balls add interest between each ghost. Make them any size you like (ours are about 1 inch in diameter).

candy corn pincushion

These small felt pincushions will be appreciated by anyone who sews or wants a festive way to display jewelry pins.

2   6 × 5-inch pieces each white and brown felt
1   6 × 5-inch piece orange felt
Quick-setting craft glue
White thread
Polyester stuffing

1. Scan or copy the patterns on page 249 and print them out. For each pincushion, cut a whole triangle from one piece of white felt and one piece of brown. Use the cut-up pattern to create the stripes: Use brown for the bottom stripe, then create the middle stripe with orange felt. Cut the top strip from white felt.

2. Spread quick-setting craft glue on the large white triangle. Position the brown stripe over the bottom section and press into place. Repeat with orange and white stripes, using the photo as your guide.

3. With the striped side up, lay the white triangle on the large brown triangle. Sew them together along the edges, leaving a small opening on one side. Fill with stuffing, then sew the edges together to close.

haunt
your house

Decorations to spruce up your rooms and make a party feel fun and festive.

HELP YOURSELF

No one says you have to dispense treats from the same bowl year after year. Why not try a new way to package the goodies you give at the door? Here are eight quick-and-easy ideas—each sure to give your offerings a whole new spirit.

basket case

Fashion a hollowed-out pumpkin into a pretty basket by adding a handle of cut vines. Any backyard vine with stiff stems will do. Clean out the pumpkin and let it sit for about 24 hours to dry before filling it with treats. Bend the vines into a handle and secure to the pumpkin with wire poked into each side.

KEEP ON TRUCKIN'

Entertain your wee guests with a dump truck full of
wrapped candies. Look for vintage ones at antiques stores,
or use a new one repurposed from the playroom.
A Halloween sticker is the company logo on the cab door.

Pretty Holdall

Look for interesting containers at home furnishings stores, discount retailers, and import stores. This wire umbrella is a decorative item that can also hold foil-wrapped candies on a front-hall bench.

You'll find an umbrella similar to this at handcrafttexas.com.

TRAY CHIC

Use a vintage tray with dividers—or in this case a drawer from a hardware-store case—to display your offerings. Due to lead paint concerns, be sure to fill any vintage vessel with wrapped candies only.

These foil-wrapped pumpkin candies shown are from Granite State Candy Shoppe (nhchocolates.com).

STAND ALONE

Set a tiered server—often used to display cakes or biscuits at high tea—on a table to keep lollipops and loose candies within reach. If you have an old server you don't use often, consider spraying it with black paint to better match the Halloween mood. Be sure to use a paint that is nontoxic when dry, such as Plasti-Kote®, which also does not contain lead.

Halloween candy starts filling the shelves of stores such as Target and Wal-Mart in September. For other stores selling holiday candies, see Resources, page 256.

HOLE IN ONE

Choose a gourd or pumpkin with a deep well in the top and trim off the stem to make a ready dish for loose chocolate-coated sesame seeds, roasted pumpkin seeds, or candy.

FACE THE FACTS

Repurpose a garden planter—such as this one from my collection with eerie faceted faces—to hold candies. Make sure to clean it thoroughly, and use a food-safe liner, such as a plastic bowl or bag, if you plan fill it with unwrapped candies.

HUMBLE ABODE

Turn a dollhouse, new birdhouse, or any kind of shelter-style
accessory into a spooky witch's lair. Paint the house with black
and dark green paints, then prop a witch figurine at the door.
Tuck candies into the windows and doors.

paper moon

Infuse your home with the moon's luminous mystery with these paper-based decorations. Some are inspired by Victorian-era folding techniques, while others make use of modern technologies. Get all the supplies you need at craft and party-supply stores, then let the bold, black-and-white creations—reminiscent of the pale orb in the inky sky—inspire you. You'll find the patterns for these projects beginning on page 250, or you can download them from matthewmeadstyle.com.

watch the CLOCK

Add a temporary decoration to an antique mantel clock by placing a moon face over the clock dial (you can photocopy this image from page 251). Use double-sided tape to secure.

moon man

Ply the grade-school technique of papier-mâché to create this smiling fellow. Use a balloon as a form for the moon. Just blow it up and wrap it in newspaper strips soaked in papier-mâché medium (available at craft stores, or see the recipe on page 250). When dry, pop the balloon with a pin, and paint the ball with white or cream acrylic paint. Cut eyes, nose, and mouth (see pattern on page 250) out of black construction paper and affix with white craft glue. Rest the moon on an old garden finial or sturdy water goblet. To make a headdress (as pictured on page 161), twist a stem out of paper, and attach paper leaves to complete the illusion.

golden GLOW

Re-create the effect of moonlight by adding quarter-moon candies to simple white candles. Use a small ball of Tacky Wax® (from the craft store) to adhere the sugar-icing treat to ball, square, or pillar-shape candles. Remember, never leave a burning candle unattended.

To purchase sugar-icing moon candies, visit chandlerscakeandcandy.com.

163

moonshine

Fold tight, crisp pleats in four pieces of scrapbook paper, which is sold in packages at craft stores. Sharpen the pleats by running a straightedge, such as a credit card, along the folds. Pinch one end of the folded paper and open the other end slightly so it resembles a fan. Arrange the four fans in quadrants to form a circle, and use clear tape to secure the seams and the center. Using more clear tape, add a moon face (page 251) to the middle. Then use a glitter pen to add sparkle to the creases. Finally, poke a small hole in the top of the medallion and string a hanging thread through.

HOME PLATE

Save a few paper plates from your Halloween party to fashion a decorative ceiling medallion. Using scalloped-edge scissors, trim the edges of two dinner plates—one white and one black—and a white dessert plate. Center the black dinner plate atop the white dinner plate and glue together with white craft glue. In the center of the white dessert plate, create a black design using a spiral drawing tool such as Spirograph.® When finished, stack the smaller plate on the others, and glue with white craft glue. Center a black painted button in the middle. Hang the medallion from the ceiling with black twine.

STRING ALONG

Starting with a length of black cording, thread large wooden beads—painted black with acrylic paint—at various intervals. For the paper coils, cut triangles from patterned scrapbook paper (use template on page 251). Starting on side A, roll the triangles around a pencil for a tight coil. Gently unroll the coil, add a strip of clear tape along side A, and string the coils onto the cord between beads.

NIGHT LIGHTS

Drape the mantel with a paper garland fashioned from scrapbook papers and black beads. Secure the center of the garland with clear tape, and display it with a smiling

moonight
welcome

Greet guests with a unique door hanging. Start with a piece of black foam core from the craft or office supply store. Punch two holes in the upper corners, using an ice pick or awl. Attach the paper moon (see page 251) using decoupage medium (such as Mod Podge®) and add a message. Thread a twisted wire into the holes for hanging, and embellish with a string and beads if desired.

cameo appearance

Fill black-and-white paper bags with takeaway treats for guests. Dress them up with a moon-face cameo tied on with black cording and beads. Shop for the treat bags at stationery and party stores, and look for similar cameos in the jewelry-making or notions sections of craft stores and fabric stores.

SWIZZLE STICK
wrappers

To make these paper packets, assemble scrapbook papers and color photocopies of old handwritten letters. These come from pages of a journal picked up at an antique sale. Fold then cut and tape the packets. Trim the top edge with decorative scrapbook scissors. Insert candy swizzle sticks (see *Resources*, page 256) and tie on a pretty ribbon.

paper PINWHEEL

Replicating the pattern on page 252, cut and fold two layers of patterned scrapbook paper into this delightfully low-tech toy. Secure the center with a sturdy straight pin or small nail pushed into the end of a black-painted wood dowel.

SPIR-O HANGING

Personalize a tissue-paper medallion from the party-supply store to hang above your guests. Fan out the medallion and set aside. Decorate paper plates with Spirograph® designs and use scalloped-edge scissors to trim the edges. Hot-glue the plates to the center of the medallion.

PAPERBACK
WRITER

Choose an old paperback from a used book store, and fold each page into the spine, creasing the fold with a straightedge as you go. As you fold the pages, the book will expand until it forms a cylinder. Secure the covers together in the back with a bead of hot glue. Photocopy the moon face (page 251), cut it out, and hot glue it to the folded book pages.

moon phases

Highlight the beautiful phases of the moon in a captivating arrangement of candy-filled plant pots. Coat the terra-cotta pots with black latex paint, let dry, then use a craft-store decoupage medium to adhere moon illustrations. Set up a buffet by filling the pots with black licorice and jelly beans and white marshmallows and mints.

Fun House

Spookify your house with items you already
have: old sheets, paper muffin cups, eggs,
and marshmallows become mummies, witches,
ghosts and more. Cleverly arranged in creepy
vignettes, they're sure to startle!

HANGING GHOSTIES

We've always felt there must be another use for pleated paper cupcake cups, and finally we discovered that they make amusing ghostly spirits. Use jumbo or king-size cupcake liners. Pierce each one with at least one pair of black paper-brad eyes (use two or three pairs to see eyes from more angles). If you can't find black brads at your craft or office-supply store, paint some brass ones with a black paint marker.

To hang them, thread a needle with monofilament or black thread, doubled and knotted, and pierce a paper liner from the inside. Pull the needle through until the liner sits on the knot. Cut the monofilament next to the needle, then tie the ends together to make a hanging loop.

To order king-size cupcake liners, visit wilton.com.

mummified
HEADS

Your friends will be spooked by these eerie mummified "severed heads." For each head, assemble a 14- or 18-inch paper lantern according to the package directions. With scissors, clip into the edge of an old white sheet at 2-inch intervals. Tear the sheet into strips (one queen-size sheet yields enough strips to wrap 4 lanterns). Attach one end of a strip to the top of a lantern with white masking tape, then wrap the strip repeatedly around the lantern and secure the other end with tape. Repeat with more strips as needed. Copy or scan and print the eye patterns on page 252 and use them to cut out the eyes from black felt (or create your own eyes). Affix them to the cloth cover with craft glue. Put eyes on the backs of the heads too, if you like.

To order paper lanterns, visit pearlriver.com.

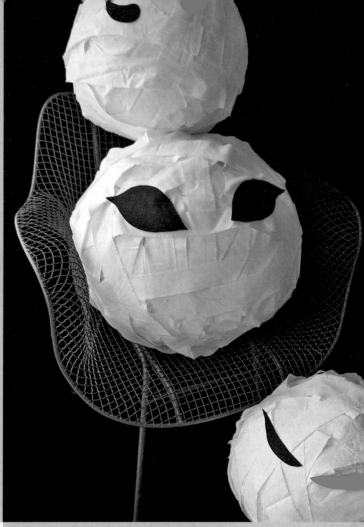

OPTICAL ILLUSION

An offering of edible eyeballs isn't an everyday treat, but this is Halloween and these eyeballs are marshmallows. To be really ghoulish, you can roast them over a fire and watch them weep! Remove large or mini marshmallows from their packages. Allow them to air-dry for about 1 hour so their surface hardens slightly. Use a black food marker (from a cake-decorating shop) to draw a variety of pupils or eyes on single or paired marshmallows. Tuck the eyeballs onto a wire tree form, which you can find in a craft or Christmas store.

For a wire tree similar to this one, go to handcrafttexas.com (be sure to mention Matthew Mead's Monster Book of Halloween to avoid the normal $50 minimum purchase).

173

poiso

MEASURING IN   MENTS

174

GHOSTIES everlasting

Classic 7-minute frosting doesn't look as sweet when piped into eggcups and embellished with candy eyes.

1½ cups sugar
⅓ cup cold water
2 egg whites
¼ teaspoon cream of tartar or 2 teaspoons light corn syrup
1 teaspoon vanilla extract (omit if not eating)
   Plastic food storage bag
   Small sugar candy eyes, 2 for each ghost
   Eggcups, cordial glasses, or any small dish or bowl

To make the frosting:

1. Combine the sugar, water, egg whites, and cream of tartar in the top of a double boiler. Using an electric mixer on low speed, beat the ingredients for 30 seconds to combine.

2. Boil a small amount of water in the bottom of the double boiler. Place the top part of the double boiler onto the bottom part. Cook the frosting on medium heat, beating constantly with the mixer on high, for about 7 minutes or until the frosting forms stiff peaks when the beaters are lifted. Remove the top of the double boiler from the bottom, and if using the vanilla extract, stir it in with a spoon or rubber spatula. Beat the frosting for 2 or 3 minutes more or until it is spreadable. Allow the frosting to cool until it is slightly warm or at room temperature.

To make the ghosties

Spoon the frosting into a plastic food storage bag, then snip off one corner of the bag, creating a ¼-inch opening. Referring to the photo, pipe the frosting into the eggcups one at a time. Applying pressure to the bag, squeeze out enough frosting to fill the cup. Gradually decrease the pressure as you slowly lift the bag until the ghostie is the desired size. Stop the pressure and lift off the bag. Press the candy eyes into position (use tweezers for better control). Once dry, wrap each ghostie in its container in tissue paper and store in a cool, dry place.

Makes 4 cups frosting, enough for about 8 ghosties. The frosting becomes rock hard if left to air-dry for 2 weeks. You can eat them when fresh if you wish or save them for decorations in the future.

176

WICKED WITCH STOCKIN[GS]

Everyone knows a witch's toes are as sharply poin[ted]
Here's how to make socks to fit.

2 skeins (3.5 ounces/220 yards each) white worsted
2 skeins (3.5 ounces/220 yards each) black worsted
size 4 (3.5mm) double-pointed needles
size 6 (4.5mm) double-pointed needles

1. Use a standard worsted-weight sock pattern (24 s
32 rows equal 4 inches/10 cm in stockinette stitch o
needles). Calf: Using white yarn and size 4 needles,
following the directions for the largest size in your s
Work the ribbing in the round as indicated until the
measures 1½ inches from the beginning; change to
and size 6 needles.

2. Continue to follow the pattern, changing colors
1¾ inches to make stripes, until the work measure
inches from the beginning, ending with a complet[e]

3. Heel: Change to black and work the heel
as indicated in the pattern.

4. Foot: Work as established for 11 inches.
Count the stitches, divide in half, place a
marker at the beginning of the next round
and halfway across it.

5. Toe: Next round: K2tog, work to next
marker, K2tog. Next 5 rounds: work even.
Continue in this manner to decrease 2 sts
every sixth round until 12 sts remain; then
decrease every fifth round until 4 sts remain.
Cut the yarn and thread it through the 4 sts;
pull tight and pass the cut end to the inside.
Repeat for the second sock.

EGGS IN DISGUISE

Here's a funny way to serve soft-boiled or
hard-cooked eggs for Halloween breakfast.
(You can also use blown shells for a
nonperishable display.)

To dress the eggs:

Trace the mask and hat patterns on page 253.
Cut them out and trace as many egg disguises
as desired on black construction paper. To
make a mask, cut out the pattern, using a
craft knife for the eyeholes. Poke a hole at
each side of the mask with a needle, and
thread a knotted string through each hole.
Position the mask on a hard- or soft-cooked
egg, then tie the strings together at the back
of the egg. To make a hat, form the top into
a cone, overlapping and taping as indicated.
Cut tabs around the inside of the brim as
indicated. Fold up the tabs and tape or glue to
the inside of the cone.

To display:

We used an old-fashioned egg carrier that we
found at a flea market, but you can display
these masked eggs however you like: Rest the
eggs atop large spools of thread or in a gray
cardboard egg carton. Or fill a basket with
black excelsior (soft shredded wood used as
packing material) to make a cozy nest.

wall eyes

Ask your guests to name the creatures staring out from this disconcerting display: give an award for the most imaginative answer. To make the eyes, assemble assorted white plates in pairs. Then copy or scan and print the eyes on page 254, resizing as needed. Attach eyes to plates with double-stick tape. Or paint eyes on plates freehand using acrylic paint and a small paintbrush. Hang the plates with plate hangers, which you can get in any craft or hardware store.

180

W
Get p
black
magi
and c
a stri
costu
knitt
broo
bird
com

paper bag brooms

Line an empty coffee can with aluminum foil and fill it halfway with candy. Place the can in a brown paper lunch bag. Wrap six or seven thin 14-inch twigs together around their middle with 1 yard of twine, tying to secure; wrap again near each end with an additional yard of twine. Insert the twig handle into the candy in the can; then fill the can with additional candy, mounding at the top. Gather the bag around the handle and tie with a 1-foot piece of twine. Cut the bottoms out of two brown paper lunch bags, then cut the lower portion of each into strips about 4½ inches deep and ½ inch wide. One at a time, slide the cut-up bags over the first one, gather the top around the handle and tie with a piece of twine. Wrap 1 yard of twine around the "bristles" at the top of the can. Support from the bottom when moving.

POSH WITCH'S HAT

Craft stores and costume shops offer a selection of witch hats at Halloween. For a table decoration or to wear, buy one and dress it up with a purple velvet band and a rhinestone buckle. To make the band, measure the hat around the base of the crown and add several inches for an overlap. Measure the inside height of your buckle. Add 1 inch to each dimension and cut two pieces of velvet to this size. Place them right sides together and sew around all edges, leaving an opening for turning. Turn right side out. Slide the buckle onto one end. Place the sash on the hat as shown, and attach with hot glue or craft glue.

FRIGHT NIGHT SPAGHETTI PARTY

A pasta buffet makes a Halloween bash easy on the host and gives guests the chance to assemble a plate of Spider Spaghetti. You'll get giggles from partygoers gobbling up cheese sandwiches with fangs and skewers loaded with cheesy ghosts. Arrange dinner offerings on a sideboard draped with an orange cloth. Hang a black curtain behind the table to create a dramatic backdrop.

mood setters

Sometimes it's the little things that make the holiday difference. Waxy Halloween candles are delightful table toppers. Dishes collected from garage sales or import stores are a budget-friendly way to reinforce your color scheme. And don't underestimate the eerie power of a well-placed plastic bird.

TWIGGY tree

Anchored in an orange bucket, a spray of branches becomes a festive tabletop tree. Trim slender branches from a backyard tree, collect fallen ones, or purchase twigs from the floral aisle of the craft store, then skewer them into a block of foam inserted in the bucket. Hide the foam with a helping of cookies. Hang orange glass balls, fuzzy little pumpkins, and vintage paper motifs (downloaded from matthewmeadstyle.com) as ornaments.

Orange ornaments are a seasonal item carried by import and home-decorating stores. You can also find them online at christmascentral.com.

POP art

Fashion personalized Halloween poppers—the popular British party gift filled with candy and small tokens—by covering blank ones from the party supply store with orange wrapping paper. Twist the paper and tie with black thread or cording. Wrap a band around the middle and glue on a holiday motif. You can download this jack-o'-lantern from matthewmeadstyle.com.

FURRY LITTLE GUY

Turn a chubby chenille pipe cleaner into a little jack-o'-lantern for your twig tree. Trim a 1½-inch length of an orange pipe cleaner into a round ball shape using small scissors. Use the wire stem to secure a button to the bottom. Thread a piece of green floral wire around the top of the wire stem and twirl into "vines." Using an X-Acto knife, cut features out of black electrical tape and stick on.

To purchase pipe cleaners like these, look for 15 mm chenille "stems" at an art supply or craft store. Or visit dickblick.com.

LIGHTS UP!

Highlight the creamy ice cream dessert on a console table. A string of globe lights, fitted with orange and clear bulbs, draws attention to the table. Paint a large garden ornament, such as this fiberglass sundial, black and hang it on the wall. (You could also look for molded ceiling medallions at the home center to paint black and hang.)

ring of fliers

Wrap black-and-white ribbons around colorful cloth napkins. Buy similar napkins at a party supply store, or sew your own from orange and black cotton fabric. Secure the ribbons with a stitch or two, then use hot glue to affix plastic bugs from the childrens' toys bin at the craft store.

WALL HANGING

Cast a pall over your gathering by hanging black-painted brackets or sconces on the wall and showcasing ghoulish ornaments. This sconce is a thrift-store find; you can also find paintable wood brackets at the craft store. Feature a white-chocolate candy skull like the one pictured here.

Look for seasonal items like this candy skull at stores such as Target (target.com).

FRIGHTFUL DELIGHTS

skewered snacks

Create festive and fun appetizer skewers for guests to nibble. Cut raw veggies, such as peppers and cucumbers into jagged shapes, then thread them onto bamboo skewers with grape tomatoes and Cheese Ghosts. To make the Cheese Ghosts, use a paring knife or cookie cutter to cut the shape out of ¼-inch-thick slices of firm white cheese, such as cheddar, Monterey Jack, or mozzarella. For the eyes, stick cloves, black peppercorns, or allspice berries into the cheese—just remove them before young children grab hold.

WITCH'S BREW

Quench guests' thirst with this fizzy punch that looks ominous but is harmlessly refreshing.

1   pint lime sherbet
4   cups milk
4   cups ginger ale
Few drops of green food coloring (optional)

1. Scoop the sherbet into a pitcher or punch bowl and let sit for about 15 minutes until it starts to soften.

2. Use a wooden spoon to break up the sherbet. Add milk; stir until smooth.

3. Add the ginger ale; stir well.

4. If a brighter green color is desired, add food color.

Makes about 20 ½-cup servings

Bread That Bites

Make clever and delicious garlic bread sandwiches to pair with the pasta entrees. The twist? Delightful seaweed fangs!

1   cup mayonnaise
1   cup grated Parmesan cheese
1   clove garlic, minced
12 French bread dinner rolls
Butter
2   tablespoons fresh basil leaves or
    2 teaspoons dried
1   sheet of nori seaweed (from an Asian or
    gourmet food store), cut into triangles

1. Preheat broiler.

2. Mix mayonnaise, cheese, and garlic in a mixing bowl. Set aside.

3. Slice rolls in half lengthwise. Spread with butter and then arrange halves cut side up on a cookie sheet. Broil for a few minutes until bread is toasted.

4. Spread cheese-mayonnaise mixture on bread halves and broil again until the mixture is puffy and golden brown, about 3 minutes.

5. Sprinkle halves with basil. Assemble sandwich halves with nori triangles in the middle, points facing out.

Makes 12 servings

back-from-the-dead salad

Fill a salad platter with healthy greens as well as zombielike eyeballs formed with mozzarella balls, hard-boiled eggs, and goat cheese-stuffed tomatoes.

1. Tear up two heads of Boston or Bibb lettuce and toss lightly with Italian-style dressing or vinaigrette.

2. For the skulls, cut mouth stitches, nostrils, and eye circles out of sheets of nori (dried seaweed available at an Asian or gourmet food store) using an X-Acto knife. Press them onto balls of fresh mozzarella.

3. For the stuffed tomatoes, hollow out cherry or grape tomatoes and remove the seeds. Fill with goat cheese and dot with a black peppercorn or allspice berry.

4. To make a salad "face," prepare hard-cooked eggs and stick on nori triangles for eyeballs. Set the eggs in circles of red onion. Use a peeler to slice a strip of carrot, and place between the eggs for a nose.

5. To serve, pair the platter with a cutting board and knife so guests can cut portions of the cheese skulls.

skeletal fingers

Roast some white asparagus spears, and tell your guests they are the appendages of previous party guests. If this delicate vegetable isn't available in your local grocery store, substitute green or yellow string beans.

1   pound white asparagus spears, rinsed and trimmed
2   cloves garlic, minced
Kosher salt to taste
Freshly ground black pepper to taste
½   lemon for squeezing
Fresh thyme leaves (optional)
Olive oil

1. Preheat oven to 400°F. Line a roasting pan with foil and drizzle with olive oil.

2. Place asparagus in pan and drizzle liberally with olive oil. Roll the spears back and forth until they are completely coated.

3. Sprinkle on minced garlic, salt, and pepper.

4. Roast for 8 to 10 minutes, until lightly browned and tender when pierced with a fork.

5. Remove from oven, squeeze fresh lemon juice over top, and garnish with thyme leaves if using.

Makes 4 servings

spider spaghetti

Encourage guests to play with their food. Pierce holes in red-pepper quarters using a plastic drinking straw. Let guests use the peppers as the backs of spiders, the spots as eyes, and fettuccine strands as legs.

1   pound spaghetti, cooked and drained
½   pound fettuccine, cooked and drained
16   ounces marinara sauce
2   red peppers, seeded and quartered

For the meatballs:

1½   pounds fresh ground turkey
1   small sweet onion, diced
2   teaspoons fresh oregano, chopped
2   teaspoons fresh basil, chopped
2–3 garlic cloves, minced
1   teaspoon salt
1   teaspoon freshly ground black pepper
3   large eggs
1¾   cups seasoned bread crumbs
1   cup heavy cream
½   cup olive oil
1   tablespoon butter

1. Preheat oven to 375°F.

2. Mix turkey, onion, fresh herbs, garlic, salt, and pepper in a large mixing bowl until well combined.

3. Add eggs, bread crumbs, and cream to the meat mixture and combine. Form into 2-inch balls.

4. In a large skillet, heat olive oil and butter over medium heat until the butter turns golden brown, about 5 minutes, stirring frequently.

5. Turn up the heat to medium-high. Add meatballs in batches of five to seven meatballs, depending on pan size, and brown on all sides. Repeat until all meatballs are browned.

6. Place meatballs in the oven on a shallow roasting pan. Bake for 10 to 15 minutes, until the internal temperature reaches 165°F.

7. Mix meatballs with sauce and place on pasta. Top meatball with pepper "spider back" and add fettuccine "legs."

Makes about 8 servings

sorcerer's pasta

Cast a spell on diners with a creamy noodle dish that includes easy-to-find ingredients.

Butter
1   pound mini-wagon-wheel pasta, cooked and drained
1   tablespoon olive oil
3   garlic cloves, minced
½   cup sweet onion, chopped
½   teaspoon salt
¼   teaspoon freshly ground pepper
1   cup frozen peas
½   cup grated Parmesan cheese
½   cup whole-milk ricotta cheese
3   cups half-and-half
2   tablespoons fresh parsley, chopped
8   ounces thick-sliced deli ham, cut into star shapes with a
    cookie cutter
¾   cup fresh bread crumbs
½   cup Fontina cheese, crumbled

1. Preheat oven to 350°F. Place pasta in a buttered 2-quart casserole dish.

2. Heat olive oil in a large skillet over medium-high heat. Add garlic and onion and cook until fragrant, stirring constantly for about 30 seconds. Add salt, pepper, and peas, and cook until peas are hot, about 2 minutes. Remove from heat.

3. Stir in Parmesan cheese, ricotta cheese, half-and-half, parsley, and ham. Simmer until thick, about 5 minutes. Pour over pasta in casserole dish and top with bread crumbs and Fontina cheese.

4. Bake for 20 to 25 minutes until bubbly. Garnish with mint leaves.

Makes about 8 servings

frozen decadence

Let your imagination drive the ingredients of this simple frozen cake. Assemble ice cream sandwiches of any flavor and top with your favorite chocolate candies. You can even size it to fit any size pan and make any number of layers to satisfy your particular crowd.

12 ice cream sandwiches
4 cups whipped topping
1 cup Peanut M&M's®, crushed (set aside ½ cup)
3 Butterfinger® candy bars, crushed
½ cup chocolate syrup

1. On a plate that will fit in your freezer, layer 6 ice cream sandwiches in pairs. Spread a thin layer of whipped topping over sandwiches, about 1 cup. Sprinkle on half the crushed peanut candies and candy bars.

2. Layer 6 more sandwiches crosswise atop the first layer, log cabin style. Spread on another cup of whipped topping, and sprinkle on remaining crushed candies.

3. Construct a third layer of sandwiches, facing the same way as the first layer.

4. Spread remaining 2 cups of whipped topping over the top and down the sides. Drizzle with chocolate syrup.

5. Cover with plastic wrap and freeze for at least 3 hours. Garnish with remaining M&M's. It can be stored, covered, for up to a month in the freezer.

Makes 8 to 10 servings

Frog & Toad Festivities

Children will get a kick out of this amphibian-theme shindig. Turn your pad into party central with green-tinted desserts, dip that looks like pond scum, and plenty of hopping hosts.

amphibious atmosphere

Round out the party theme by using dinnerware decorated with green motifs. For a temporary investment, look for paper plates in grassy hues, or use everyday white place settings dressed up with green accents, such as green-striped or polka-dotted tablewear and a small frog figurine.

FROG AND TOAD
favor

HOP ALONG TREAT

FROGGY Favor

Make cute giveaways for your guests by filling plastic pencil cases with green PixyStix®.
Download this tag from matthewmeadstyle.com, or make your own from a photo of a frog
figurine. Wrap the package with grosgrain ribbon.

stop by our pad for a
PARTY
food, friends, fun

WEAR YOUR FAVORITE HALLOWEEN COSTUME

HOP ON over
Set the date with friends and neighbors by delivering these charming invitations designed to hang from doorknobs or mailboxes. Photocopy this invite (page 255) or download it from matthewmeadstyle.com. Finish with twine for the tie.

TO THE LETTER

Spell out the party theme using alphabet-shaped tater tots. These are made by OreIda® and are available in most grocery stores. If you can find only plain potato snacks, use the green-tinted ranch dressing dip to spell out a message. For green-tinted letters, fill a resealable plastic bag with dip, snip off a corner, and use the bag to pipe the words onto a tray or platter.

TICKLISH TOAD

Fill a goofy toad garden planter with candies that suit the color scheme. Insert a plastic food-safe container and fill with candies, such as M&M's®, which are available in any hue and can be customized with Halloween sayings. Visit mymms.com to order.

marshy menu

Polliwog Punch

Pond Sludge Dip

Baby Burgers

Hop-Along Cake

Tasty Tadpoles

Cutest Whoopie
Pies Ever

POLLIWOG PUNCH

Tempt guests with fizzy lemonade tinted fresh frog green. Serve it up in a large fish bowl.

8 kiwis
1 cup superfine sugar
¾ cup freshly squeezed lemon juice
1 liter seltzer water, chilled
3 drops green food color

1. Peel kiwi. Slice two crosswise and set aside. Puree remaining six in a blender. Strain to remove seeds.

2. In a large pitcher, combine sugar and lemon juice. Stir until sugar is dissolved.

3. Stir in strained kiwi. Cover and chill in refrigerator for at least an hour.

4. Just before serving, stir in seltzer water and food coloring. Serve over ice and garnish with sliced kiwi.

Makes about 8 ½ cup servings

POND SLUDGE DIP

Let kids get messy dipping blue-corn tortilla chips into this delicious bean dip. They don't have to know it's packed with fiber and vegetables. For a fun serving idea, place a frog figurine or saltshaker in the middle of the "pond."

2   tablespoons olive oil
½   cup carrot, chopped
½   cup celery, stringy ribs removed, chopped
½   cup onion, chopped
1   dash garlic salt
3   14-ounce cans low-sodium black beans, rinsed
1   cup frozen corn
2   cups chicken broth
1   24-ounce bag blue sesame corn chips

1. Heat olive oil in a large saucepan or stockpot. Add carrot, celery, onion, and garlic salt, and cook on medium heat until carrots are tender, about 8 minutes.

2. Add all remaining ingredients. Bring to a boil, then lower the temperature and simmer, covered, for 20 minutes, stirring occasionally.

3. Let cool, then puree with a hand blender until still slightly chunky. Serve with chips.

Makes enough to serve 8 to 12 people

BaBY Burgers

Hand out some kid-size sliders made with ground-up flies, also known as healthy ground turkey. Substitute whole-wheat rolls for even more nutrition.

24 ounces lean ground turkey, pressed into 3-inch patties
½ pound cheddar cheese, sliced into 3 × 3-inch squares
12 mini hamburger buns or dinner rolls
    light mayonnaise or ketchup (optional)

1. Broil or grill burgers until internal temperature is 165 degrees, about 8 to 10 minutes.

2. Top burgers with cheese and cook 1 more minute to melt cheese.

3. Place burgers in buns spread with mayonnaise and/or ketchup if desired.

Makes 12 burgers

HOP-ALONG cake

Celebrate the holiday in style with a show-stopping frog cake. Bake a cake from the mix of your choice in a frog-shaped pan. Cover it with a coat of green-tinted cake frosting, smoothing the frosting as you go. To decorate, outline the features of the frog with black frosting piped from a decorating bag fitted with a #4 tip. Fill in with green frosting rosettes, created by using a decorating bag fitted with a #35 tip. Form the eyes and tongue out of frosting, as pictured, or roll out colored ready-to-use fondant for these features. Green fondant circles are placed like freckles.

To purchase Wilton's vintage Big Frog cake pan, look on ebay.com. Or, check wilton.com for ideas on forming other pans, such as the Animal Crackers pan, into a frog shape.

TASTY TADPOLES

Offer up a batch of small green chocolate frogs as snacks or take-home gifts. To make your own, purchase a candy mold and use melting chocolate, such as Wilton's CandyMelts®, from the grocery store or craft store. If necessary, tint the chocolate with candy-making tints.

To purchase green milk-chocolate frogs, visit candytech.com. To purchase a frog-shaped candy mold, go to candymoldcentral.com.

cutest **WHOOPIE PIES** ever

Bake delicious mini whoopie pies using green food color to tint the cakes. Serve the pies on top of green ice cream cones.

Cakes:

- ½ cup (1 stick) butter, softened
- ⅔ cup sugar
- 3 eggs
- ¼ cup whole milk
- ½ teaspoon vanilla extract
- 1½ cup flour
- 1½ teaspoon baking powder
- 6 drops Cake Craft Avocado Paste Food Color

Filling:

- 7 ounces cream cheese, softened
- 3 tablespoons butter
- 1 pound powdered sugar
- 2 teaspoons vanilla extract
- 18 green ice cream cones (optional)

For assembly:

- 36 Golden Oreo® Cakesters
- 36 medium-size candy icing eyes
- 9 pieces strawberry- or cherry-flavor LaffyTaffy®, cut into slender strips

Bake the Cakes

1. Preheat the oven to 350°F.

2. In a mixing bowl, cream the butter and sugar together until pale and fluffy. Add the eggs one by one, beating well in between. Add the milk and vanilla.

3. In a separate small bowl, sift together the flour and baking powder. Add to the wet ingredients and mix until there are no lumps.

4. Add food color and mix.

5. Line cookie sheet with parchment paper. Place tablespoon-size scoops of batter on paper, spacing at least 2 inches apart. Use your fingers to shape batter into a circle.

6. Bake for 7 to 8 minutes. Let cool.

Make the Filling

Place all the ingredients for the filling into a medium-size bowl. Mix well with an electric beater.

Assemble Whoopie Pies

1. Using an angled metal spatula, spread filling between two cakes.

2. Use filling to affix two Cakesters to the top of each whoopie pie. Use more filling to attach candy icing eyes.

3. Stick a curled LaffyTaffy strip into the filling to make the tongue. Place assembled pie on a green ice cream cone if desired.

Makes 18 whoopie pies

Purchase candy icing eyes from sugarcraft.com.

Purchase Avocado Paste Food Color from cakecraft.net.

owl-oween party

You'll appreciate the easy preparations for this fun fall party. Make our owl cookies and a fantastic "feathered" cake, and serve drinks in wise-looking bottles. Have a hoot with our owl graphics reminiscent of the 1970s. Download the patterns from matthewmeadstyle.com or create your own owl-inspired motifs.

soDa POP OWLS

Juice, soda, or punch—it's more fun to drink just about anything from a decorated bottle. (We used Izze® sparkling juice bottles, because the bottle caps have cute asterisks that look like twinkling eyes, but you can paint any cap or make the eyes from polymer clay such as Fimo® or Sculpey.®) If you use bottle caps, plan ahead—you need two for every owl bottle. One 2-ounce block of clay will make six beaks or twelve eyes.

Soak the empty bottles in warm soapy water to remove the labels. Meanwhile, roll out the clay to about ¼-inch thickness. Referring to the photo, use a paring knife to cut a diamond shape about 2¼ inches long and ⅞ inch wide for each beak. (If making eyes, cut them out with a small canapé cutter and paint them with acrylic paint.) Bake the clay according to package directions. Attach the beaks and eyes to the bottles with hot glue. Using a funnel, fill the decorated bottles with juice, punch, or fruit-flavored soda. Serve with bendy straws.

WATCHFUL GARLAND

Add style and focus to your party spot by stringing these fun paper owls across a window or on the wall above your buffet. Download the motifs from matthewmeadstyle.com and print on white card stock, sizing as you wish (ours are 5¼ and 6 inches tall). Print and cut out as many as you like. With a hole punch, make a hole at the top of each owl. Thread them onto a long piece of ribbon or string, tying it at each hole as shown to keep the birds spaced at the interval you like best.

IT'S a HOOT!
Our owl-inspired recipes and crafts will set you on your way to throwing one hoot of a Halloween party. Collect trinkets and table decor (such as glasses, plates, and eggcups) all year long to add to the atmosphere. Kids will love attending this bash and helping to prepare for it too.

HOOT COOKIES

These owl cookies taste so good, they're likely to fly off the table.
Owl cookie cutters are available at baking-supply stores.

2   cups unsalted butter, softened
2   cups sugar
4   large eggs, beaten
¼   cup milk
2   teaspoons vanilla extract
4   cups all-purpose flour
½   teaspoon baking powder
1   recipe Royal Icing (page 242)
Lime green paste or gel food color
Leaf green paste or gel food color
Orange paste or gel food color

Lemon yellow paste or gel food color
Golden yellow paste or gel food color
Piping gel
Green sanding sugar
Orange sanding sugar
Yellow sanding sugar
Decorating bags with couplers
#2, #3, and #5 round tips (one
    tip for each icing color)
Small pastry brush

1. Heat the oven to 350°F. Cream the butter and sugar in a large bowl. Mix in the eggs, then the milk and vanilla. Mix the flour and baking powder in a medium-size bowl; then beat into the butter mixture until blended and smooth. Roll the dough on a lightly floured surface to ¼-inch thickness. Cut out the owl cookies and arrange on ungreased baking sheets. Bake for 8 minutes, until just golden. Transfer to wire racks to cool completely.

2. Divide the Royal Icing into two small bowls. Dilute the icing in one bowl with water until it has the consistency of thin sauce. Divide the thinned icing into three small bowls. Divide the undiluted icing into 3 small bowls. Tint one bowl of each consistency light green (a blend of lime green and leaf green food colors). Tint one bowl of each consistency orange, and one bowl of each consistency soft yellow (made by blending lemon yellow and golden yellow food colors).

3. Transfer the undiluted icings to the decorating bags. Fit a #3 tip onto a bag with thicker icing in whichever color you wish to use first. Hold the bag at an angle with the tip against the cookie and outline the perimeter. Then, using a teaspoon, flood the surface of the cookie with the same color thinned icing. Repeat with the other cookies. Let the cookies dry for one hour.

4. Referring to the photos, add other details to the cookies with the undiluted icing. Use the #5 tips for thicker lines such as the brow and eyes and the #2 tips for thinner details. Paint the forehead with piping gel and sprinkle with sanding sugar; let set, then gently invert to release any excess sugar.

Makes about 2 dozen 7-inch cookies

To order the owl cutter used here, visit victortradingco.com.

wise OWL cake

Whooo dares to eat this charmer? Everyone at your table! It's
fun to assemble from cupcakes, donuts, and oodles of frosting.

30 unfrosted cupcakes, store-bought or made from your favorite recipe
1 recipe Easy Icing (page 000)
1 tube ready-made vanilla decorating frosting (to fill donut holes)
2 chocolate-glazed sprinkle-topped donuts
2 black jelly beans

Orange gel food color
Red gel food color
Brown gel food color
Decorating bags with couplers
#199 fine-cut tip, #2 and #5 round tips
Offset spatula

1. Arrange the cupcakes in a single layer to fill a large round plate (ours is 16 inches in diameter).

2. For the beak, spoon ¾ cup Easy Icing into a small bowl. Tint with 23 drops orange food color and 10 drops red food color, mixing until blended. For the accents, spoon ¼ cup frosting into a second bowl and tint with brown food color. Tint the remaining 3 cups frosting with 30 drops of orange food color, nine drops of red food color, and six drops of brown food color.

3. Fit a decorating bag with the #199 tip. Fill the bag with orange icing. Cover the top of the assembled cupcakes with "feather" peaks as shown. For each peak, hold the bag straight up with the tip against the cake; squeeze the bag, keeping the tip in the icing until the peak forms; stop the pressure and reposition the tip for the next peak. Work from the center out, rotating the plate; refill the bag as needed.

4. Place the donut tops on the frosted cake for eyes, as shown. Pipe vanilla decorating frosting into the center of each and top with a jellybean. For the beak, use a spoon to place three dollops of frosting on the cake: Start with a largish dollop near the eyes, then add two dollops below it, each smaller than the previous. Run the spatula under hot water until heated, dry thoroughly, and use to contour the beak as shown.

5. Fit the other decorating bag with the #5 round tip. Fill the bag with the brown icing. Hold the bag at an angle and pipe the brow outline onto the cake as shown. Change the tip to the #2 round tip and pipe on the squiggle details.

Serves 25-30

mummy cooked

Celebrate big time with a theme party of rare sophistication and well-made delicacies. The mummy sets the tone for entrée and decor, while a poisonous shade of green provides an appropriate accent for the table or buffet settings. Monster pizzas, gruesome broccoli puree, and for the finale: death by chocolate. What could be more fitting?

menu

Yummy Mummy Meatloaf
Monster Pizzas
Green Gruel with Eyeballs
Bleary-Eyed Potatoes

Green Goblin Punch
Bleeding Berry Pie
Death-By-Chocolate Cakes

Start with an assortment of footed vases and a few yards of white muslin; you'll also need tape, hot glue, and black buttons (two for each vase plus one for a mouth if you like).

For each vase, snip and then tear ½ yard muslin crosswise into ½-inch-wide strips. Tape the end of one strip to the vase, then wrap around, crisscrossing as you go. Tape the other end to secure. Repeat to cover most of the vase, reserving two or three strips. Use hot glue to affix two black buttons in place for eyes, plus one for a mouth if you like. Cut one of the muslin strips into shorter pieces and tape across the top and bottom of the buttons. Wrap the remaining strips around the vase a few more times, taping as before.

TOOTHY GRIN PLATE

Who would expect plates to be screaming for their dinner? Set the table with these gaping maws; when ready to serve your meal, top them with clear glass plates. Copy or scan and print the pattern on page 253 or create your own from black construction paper. You will need two sets of teeth for each plate. Affix the teeth to plain white paper plates or china plates with double-stick tape.

SQUEAMISH NAPKIN RINGS

How inviting—a spiderweb or peeking mummy to keep napkins under control. For both, start with some plain muslin. For the spiderweb wrap, snip and then tear a 2 × 10-inch strip; wrap around a rolled napkin and tape to secure. Add a spiderweb trinket, affixing with a loop of tape if it is not self-adhesive. For the mummy wrap, snip and then tear two ¼ × 18-inch strips and two ¼ × 10-inch strips. Wrap the two longer strips around the rolled napkin, taping to secure. Use hot glue to attach two candy eyes in place. Wrap the shorter strips around, partially covering the eyes; tape to secure.

To order spiderweb decorations, visit blumchen.com.

229

Yummy Mummy Meatloaf

This mournful relic makes a silly entrée everyone will enjoy.

Meatloaf:
1½ pounds ground beef
1 egg
1 medium onion, chopped
1 cup milk
1 cup dry bread crumbs
¼ teaspoon salt
⅛ teaspoon ground black pepper
⅓ cup ketchup
2 tablespoons brown sugar
2 tablespoons prepared mustard
8 ounces pappardelle pasta
1 3-ounce mozzarella ball
1 can pitted large black olives

Sauce:
¾ cup ketchup
¾ cup water
¼ cup brown sugar
½ teaspoon prepared mustard

To make the meatloaf:

1. Heat the oven to 350°F. Lightly oil a 10 × 13-inch (or 10-inch round) baking dish. Combine the meat, egg, onion, milk, bread crumbs, salt, and pepper in a large bowl. Shape the mixture into a 10-inch round dome and place it in the baking dish. Mix the ⅓ cup ketchup, 2 tablespoons brown sugar, and 2 tablespoons prepared mustard in a small bowl until blended. Spread the mixture over the meatloaf. Bake for 1 hour. Transfer the meatloaf to a wire rack and let rest for 20 minutes.

2. Cook the pappardelle according to the package directions; drain and keep warm while meatloaf rests.

To make the sauce:

1. Combine all the ingredients in a small saucepan. Cook over medium heat, stirring, until bubbly and thickened, about 3 minutes. Keep warm until ready to serve.

2. Remove the meatloaf from the pan and place on a serving plate. Cut the mozzarella ball in half. Layer the pasta strands one by one over the meatloaf to look like a mummy's wrappings, adding the mozzarella and two olives for eyes as shown. Surround the meatloaf with more olives. Serve with the sauce on the side.

Makes 6 servings

frankenstein pizza

Run for your life or munch on this monster? Cut each shape from a packaged 10-inch pizza crust. For the guy on the right, top with pizza sauce, then scatter shredded mozzarella over the chin, neck, and shoulders. Use pitted black olives for eyes, thinly sliced zucchini for hair, a pepperoni triangle for a nose, and a larger piece of zucchini for the mouth. For the fellow on the left, top the crust with pesto, make a pepperoni hairdo, then add black olive eyes and a goat cheese frown. Bake at 375°F for 12 to 15 minutes, or until the bottom of the crust is browned and the cheese is melted.

To order the shaped cutters on these pages, go to victortradingco.com or look for similar ones at a baking-supply store.

WITCH PIZZa

She looks wicked good! Cut the shape from a packaged 12-inch pizza crust. Top with pizza sauce. Use pitted black olives for the hat and eye, red and orange pepper slices for the hatband and buckle, and thinly sliced zucchini for the hair. Shape the mouth from a peeled zucchini slice. Lightly sprinkle shredded mozzarella over the hat and hair. Bake at 375°F for 12 to 15 minutes, or until the bottom of the crust is browned and the cheese is melted.

GHOST PIZZa

Give your ghost the saddest, funniest, or scariest expression you can. Cut the shape from a packaged 10-inch pizza crust. Spread pizza sauce around the perimeter. Spread pesto over the center and top with shredded mozzarella for the face. Ring the face with cherry tomatoes, then add pitted black olive eyes and a red pepper mouth with wicked orange pepper teeth. Bake at 375°F for 12 to 15 minutes, or until the bottom of the crust is browned and the cheese is melted.

green gruel
with eyeballs

People may feel a bit wary at first glance, but this broccoli soup is delicious and the eyeball is a harmless hard-cooked egg.

3   tablespoons unsalted butter
2½ pounds broccoli, tops chopped into ½-inch florets; stalks chopped into ½-inch pieces
3   shallots, finely chopped
1   garlic clove, minced
¼   teaspoon salt
⅛   teaspoon ground black pepper
1   cup vegetable or chicken broth
½   pound grated sharp cheddar cheese (2 cups)
6   hard-cooked eggs, peeled
6   pitted black olives
Pinch freshly grated nutmeg

1. Melt 1 tablespoon of the butter in a 12-inch nonstick skillet over medium heat. Add the chopped broccoli stems, shallots, garlic, salt, pepper, and nutmeg; cook, stirring, until the shallots are tender, 3 to 5 minutes.

2. Add the broth, cover, and simmer 20 minutes, until the broccoli stalks are tender and the liquid almost evaporated. Remove from the heat, add the cheese, and toss to combine. Working in batches, transfer to a blender and puree until smooth.

3. Bring a large pot of lightly salted water to a boil. Add the florets and cook for 3 minutes. Drain and rinse under cold running water to stop the cooking.

4. Cut a notch in the side of each egg and press an olive into it. Heat broccoli puree over medium heat until just warmed through, 5 minutes. Stir in the florets and the remaining butter. Spoon the gruel into individual soup bowls and top each with an egg eye; serve immediately.

Makes 6 servings

bleary-eyed
potatoes

Mummy takes a turn for the Southwest with this spooky side dish.

12   medium Yukon gold potatoes
1   cup prepared guacamole
1   cup sour cream
½   cup mild salsa or taco sauce
24   slices cut from very large pitted black olives

1. Heat the oven to 450°F. Prick the potatoes with a fork and place directly on the rack in the oven. Bake until soft, about 1½ hours. Remove the potatoes and let stand until cool.

2. Cut each potato in half lengthwise. Spread the cut side of each with some guacamole. Top with a dollop of sour cream. Decorate with an olive slice and some salsa.

Makes 4 servings

Green GOBLIN PUNCH

A clear punch bowl shows off this potion's wonderfully evil tint. Chill the ingredients before you mix them.

1   bottle (64 ounces) white cranberry juice
1   bottle (2 liters) ginger ale
1   bottle (1 liter) orange-flavored seltzer
Green food color

Mix the cranberry juice, ginger ale, and seltzer in a punch bowl. Tint with 3 to 5 drops food color. Serve immediately.

Makes about 20 cups

BLEEDING BERRY PIE

If you feel the urge to rescue the souls who've drowned here, dig in. We've made this delicious mixed-berry filling from scratch, but if you're haunted by lack of time, purchase a blueberry pie and just add the candy eyes.

2   refrigerated piecrusts (one 15-ounce package)
2   packages (16 ounces each) frozen blueberries
1   package (16 ounces) frozen cherries
1   cup fresh or frozen cranberries
1½ cups sugar
3   tablespoons all-purpose flour
¼   teaspoon salt
¼   cup cold unsalted butter, cut into small pieces
9   pairs candy eyes in assorted sizes (from a cake-decorating store)

1. Heat the oven to 400°F. Fit one piecrust into a 9-inch pie plate.

2. Add blueberries, cherries, cranberries, sugar, flour, and salt to a large bowl and stir. Spoon the berry mixture onto the crust. Dot with the butter pieces. Top with the second crust; crimp the edges together. With a paring knife, cut six slits radiating around the center of the top crust.

3. Bake for 30 to 35 minutes, until the filling has bubbled up through the slits. Transfer to a wire rack to cool completely.

4. Just before serving, dot the top with the candy eyes in pairs as shown.

Makes 8 servings

DEATH-BY-CHOCOLATE CAKES

Give your party a deliciously chilly ending with these small frozen ice cream cakes.

1   pint chocolate ice cream
6   chocolate sponge cake cups
Chocolate Ganache (recipe follows)
Decorating sugar in the color of your choice (we used yellow)
6   candy mummy decorations

1. Remove the ice cream from the freezer and let soften for 15 minutes. Arrange the sponge cakes on a baking sheet that will fit in your freezer. Spoon some ice cream into the well of each cake, smoothing to level the top. Place in the freezer until the ice cream is firm.

2. Make the Chocolate Ganache. Remove the cakes from the freezer. Drizzle the warm ganache over them; let sit for 10 minutes. Sprinkle with decorating sugar and top with a candy. Serve or return to the freezer until ready to eat.

Chocolate Ganache
8   ounces (8 squares) semisweet or bittersweet chocolate, chopped
½   cup heavy cream
2   tablespoons light corn syrup
1   teaspoon vanilla extract
2   tablespoons softened unsalted butter

1. Place the chocolate in a medium heatproof bowl.

2. In a small saucepan over medium heat, heat the cream just to simmering. Pour the cream over the chocolate; let sit for 2 to 4 minutes. Whisk in corn syrup, vanilla extract, and butter, whisking together until the chocolate is melted and the mixture is smooth.

Serves 6

Chocolate sponge cake cups are available at grocery stores.

*For mummy candy decorations,
visit chandlerscakeandcandy.com.*

240

Bonus Patterns

These and all of the other patterns and templates used to create the projects in this book can be downloaded from matthewmeadstyle.com. We have also included a couple of basic recipes and techniques for easy Halloween planning.

ROYAL ICING

We prefer to use powdered egg whites, such as Just Whites©, for icing recipes like this one in which the egg whites are not cooked.

1	box (1 pound) confectioner's sugar	⅓	cup water
4	teaspoons powdered egg whites (not reconstituted)	1	Tablespoon fresh lemon juice
		1	teaspoon vanilla extract

In a large bowl, beat together all ingredients with an electric mixer at medium speed until just combined, about 1 minute. Increase speed to high and beat icing, scraping down side of bowl occasionally, until it holds stiff peaks, 3 to 5 minutes. Use immediately or cover surface directly with plastic wrap and refrigerate up to 2 days.

Makes about 3 cups

easy ICING

This icing will become a standby in your recipe repertoire—it's a pure shade of white, so responds well to food color.

½	cup vegetable shortening	½	teaspoon butter flavoring
1	teaspoon vanilla extract	½	teaspoon salt
½	teaspoon almond extract	4	cups confectioner's sugar

Beat the shortening, vanilla and almond extracts, butter flavoring, and salt in a large mixing bowl with an electric mixer on medium speed for 30 seconds. Slowly add 2 cups confectioner's sugar, beating well. Beat in 2 tablespoons water. Slowly add the remaining 2 cups confectioner's sugar; add 1 to 3 tablespoons more water, as needed, beating to a spreadable consistency.

Makes 4 cups

HOW TO MELT CHOCOLATE

Whether you're dipping cookies in chocolate or using it for cupcake decorations, this technique will help you melt chocolate without burning it. Be sure to set the microwave to 50 percent power each time you heat the chocolate.

Place 32 ounces milk- or dark-chocolate chips in a medium glass mixing bowl. Microwave and heat at 50 percent power for 1 minute. Stir the chips, and then heat for 30 seconds more. Stir and repeat at 30-second intervals until most of the chips are melted. The remaining chips will continue to melt after you remove the bowl from the microwave.

YELLOW cake

Moist and lightly flavored with citrus zest, this recipe is perfect for cakes or cupcakes.

2½ cups all-purpose flour, plus extra for pans
2½ teaspoons baking powder
½ teaspoon salt
⅔ cup (5⅔ ounces) unsalted butter or margarine, at room temperature
1¾ cups sugar

2 large eggs, at room temperature
1½ teaspoons vanilla extract
1¼ cups milk
2 teaspoons grated fresh orange zest or lemon zest
Shortening, as needed

1. Preheat oven to 350°F.

2. With shortening, lightly grease the bottom of the cake pan of your choosing, then line it with waxed paper or parchment paper and grease and lightly flour the bottom and sides. If you are making cupcakes, line the cups with paper liners.

3. In a medium bowl, whisk together the cups flour, the baking powder, and salt.

4. Using an electric mixer on medium to high speed, beat the butter in a large bowl for 30 seconds. With the mixer on medium speed, gradually add the sugar, about ¼ cup at a time, beating each addition 3 to 4 minutes or until well combined. Using a rubber spatula, scrape down the sides of the bowl; continue beating on medium speed for 2 minutes more, until the mixture is smooth and creamy. Add the eggs one at a time, beating for 30 seconds after each addition. Beat in the vanilla extract.

5. With the mixer on low speed and beating until just combined after each addition, beat the flour mixture into the butter mixture in three additions, alternating with two additions of the milk. Add the orange or lemon zest and, with the mixer on medium to high speed, beat the batter for 20 seconds more.

6. Using a rubber spatula, spread the batter in the prepared pans. Unless your project directions indicate otherwise, fill round, square, rectangular, or shaped pans two-thirds full; fill cupcake cups two-thirds full. Bake the cake(s) for 30 to 35 minutes; bake cupcakes for 12-15 minutes. A cake is finished when a toothpick inserted in its center comes out clean.

7. Transfer the cake in the pan to a wire rack. Cool in the pan for 10 minutes, then invert onto the rack, lift off the pan, and peel off the waxed paper. Let the cake cool completely on the wire rack. Remove cupcakes from the pans after cooling for 15 minutes.

This recipe makes a standard 8-inch or 9-inch two-layer cake, enough to serve 12 to 16 people, or 24 cupcakes

SPIRIT raisers
page 21

vampire snacks
page 57

BLACK CAT COOKIES
page 77

GLITTER JACK BASKETS
page 33

Enlarge or shrink these faces as needed to fit your baskets.

Batty Bombe
page 96

For the larger bat wings, follow the orange line; for the smaller wings, use the black template only. Enlarge or shrink as desired.

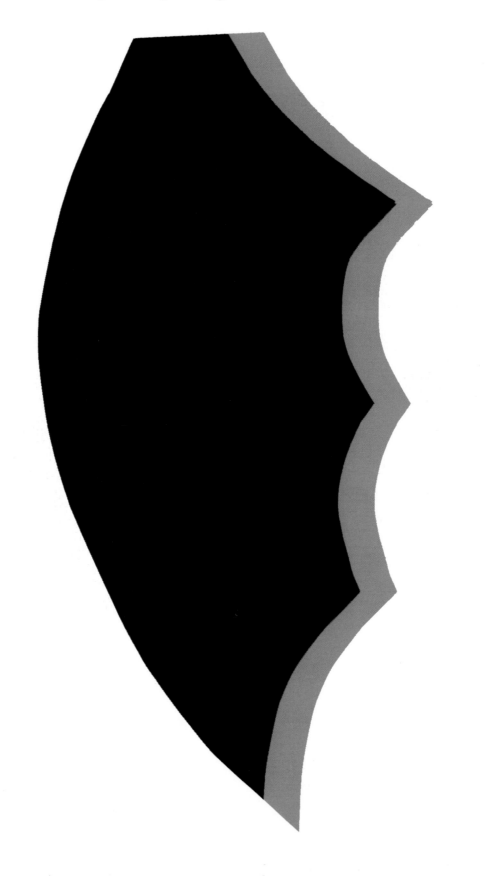

GOING BaTTY
page 124

Enlarge or shrink to fit any size pumpkin.

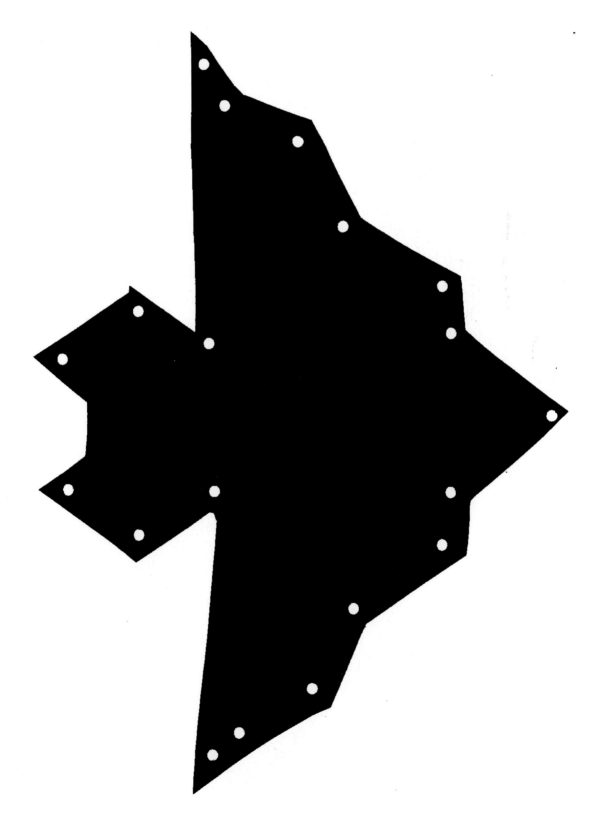

GHOST Garland
page 148

Enlarge to 200% to make 7-inch ghosts.

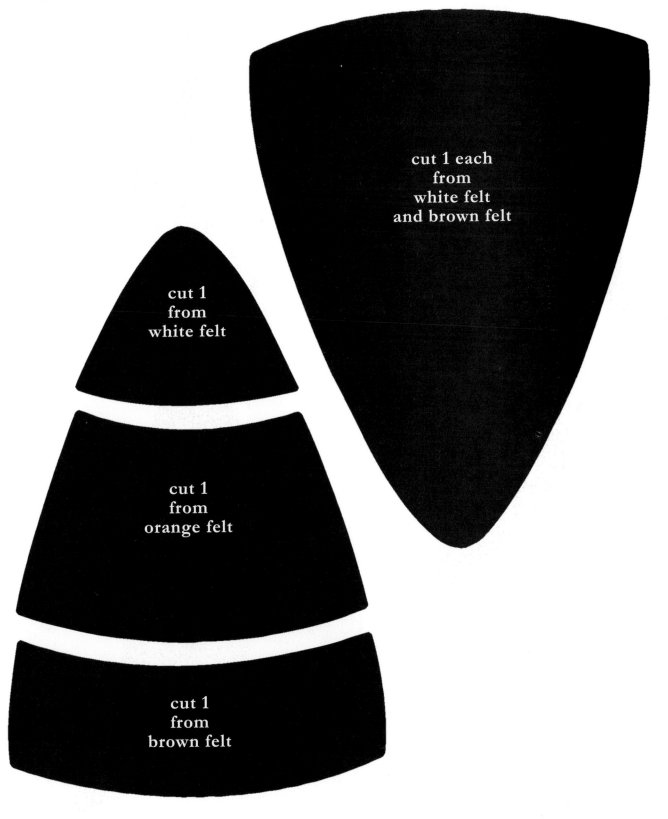

cut 1 each
from
white felt
and brown felt

cut 1
from
white felt

cut 1
from
orange felt

cut 1
from
brown felt

moon man
page 163

To make the moon enlarge this image to the size of your balloon.

papier-mâché glue

1 cup Mod Podge®
4 tablespoons water

Combine ingredients in a small mixing bowl and whisk together until smooth. Dip strips of paper in the glue, let excess drip off, and apply paper strips over the balloon form. When dry, use a pin to pop the balloon inside, then use more Mod Podge to glue on the face.

WATCH THE CLOCK
moon face
page 162

moonshine
Face
page 164

STRING ALONG
Garland page 165

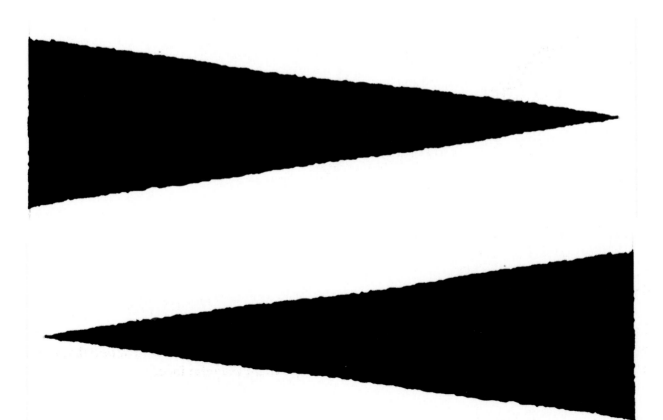

Paper PINWHEEL

page 167

mummified Heads

page 173

Enlarge or shrink as necessary to fit your lanterns.
Remember to make pairs!

TOOTHY GRIN PLATE

page 229

Enlarge or shrink as needed to fit your plates.

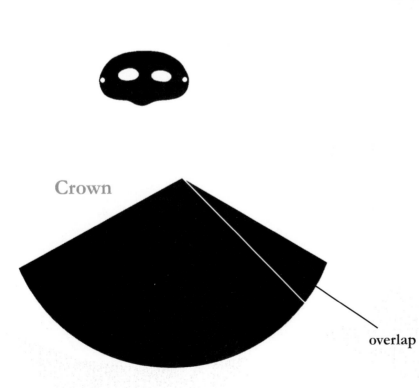

EGGS IN DISGUISE

page 177

Brim

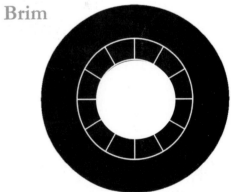

snip tabs and
fold to attach
brim to crown

Crown

overlap

waLL eyes
page 180

Enlarge or shrink as necessary to fit your plates.

more templates!

Don't forget to check matthewmeadstyle.com to download all the patterns and templates used in this book. The site is awash in inspiring ideas for every holiday and season.

stop by our pad for a

PARty

food, friends, fun

WEAR YOUR FAVORITE HALLOWEEN COSTUME

255

resources

Below are some of our favorite supply shops.

Candy and Food

Candy Tech *candytech.com*

Candy Warehouse *candywarehouse.com*

Chandler's Cake and Candy Supplies *chandlerscakeandcandy.com*

Granite State Candy Shoppe *nhchocolates.com*

Lindt Chocolates *lindtusa.com*

M&M's *mymms.com*

Nabisco *nabisco.com*

Nuts Online *nutsonline.com*

Swoozies *swoozies.com*

Party and Home Decor Supplies

Christmas Central *christmascentral.com*

Crate & Barrel *crateandbarrel.com*

ebay *ebay.com*

Hallmark *hallmark.com*

Hand Craft Texas *handcrafttexas.com*

Home Goods *homegoods.com*

iparty *iparty.com*

Kate's Paperie *katespaperie.com*

Oriental Trading *orientaltrading.com*

Pearl River *pearlriver.com*

Sur la Table *surlatable.com*

Williams-Sonoma *williams-sonoma.com*

World Market *worldmarket.com*

Baking, Crafting, and Decorating Supplies

A.C. Moore *acmoore.com*

Amazon *amazon.com*

ArtBeat *artbeatgifts.com*

Cake Craft *cakecraft.net*

Candy Mold Central *candymoldcentral.com*

Blick Art Materials *dickblick.com*

Jo-Ann Fabrics *joann.com*

Michaels *michaels.com*

Target *target.com*

Sugar Craft *sugarcraft.com*

Wal-Mart *walmart.com*

Wilton *wilton.com*